NVQ Handbook

Books in the series

Developing Human Resources
Thomson and Mabey

Management Task
Dixon

Managing an Effective Operation
Fowler and Graves

Managing Effectively
Reeves

Managing Financial Resources
Broadbent and Cullen

Managing Information
Wilson

Managing Knowledge
Wilson

Managing People
Thomson

Managing Quality
Wilson, McBride and Bell

Managing in the Single European Market
Brown

Marketing
Lancaster and Reynolds

Meeting Customer Needs
Smith

Personal Effectiveness
Murdock and Scutt

NVQ Handbook

Practical guidelines for providers and assessors

*Published in association with
the Institute of Management*

John Walton

*the Institute
of Management*

FOUNDATION

BUTTERWORTH
HEINEMANN

Butterworth-Heinemann
Linacre House, Jordan Hill, Oxford OX2 8DP
A division of Reed Educational and Professional Publishing Ltd

℞ A member of the Reed Elsevier plc group

OXFORD   BOSTON   JOHANNESBURG
MELBOURNE   NEW DELHI   SINGAPORE

First published 1996

British Library Cataloguing in Publication Data
Walton, 'John'
    NVQ handbook: practical guidelines for providers and
    assessors
    1   Vocational qualifications – Great Britain
    I.   Title II.Institute of Management
    374'.013'0941

ISBN 0 7506 2236 9

Typeset, from data supplied, by Datix International Limited, Bungay, Suffolk
Printed and bound in Great Britain by Clays Ltd, St Ives plc

Contents

Preface

This handbook is a guide for current and intending providers, assessors and verifiers of higher level S/NVQs. Its target audience includes at one end of the spectrum small specialist training organizations, and, at the other, providers of programmes in further and higher education institutions who are considering the implications for them of the emergence of higher level S/NVQs. It assumes some basic knowledge of the S/NVQ system and the structure of an S/NVQ award. However, the basic system and structure have become remarkably complicated. There are many nuances of meaning, and even points of principle, emerging which require quite a deep understanding if one is to operate effectively in the field.

As one gets into the intricacies of the system it is easy, if one is not careful, to get lost in a labyrinth of 'technical issues' and jargon, NVQ-speak, vested interests, predetermined positions and political stances which, at best, tend to confuse the basic message. On the subject of terminology alone, as with all new areas, it is amazing how much 'vocabulary' can be generated over a relatively short period of time. Lead bodies, awarding bodies, assessment centres, D units (D31–D36), elements, units, performance criteria, range statements, are just a few of the terms that players in the system have grown to know and love since 1986 when NVQs were first introduced. And for many of the terms there can be subtle shades of meaning and differences in interpretation. The distinction between the notion of competence and competency, Shirley Fletcher argues, has generated a debate reaching almost theological dimensions (1). All this can be very frustrating for people who are trying to find their way through the labyrinth. I recall a recent workshop in which, when the distinction between 'capability' and 'competence' was discussed, one delegate threw up his hands in horror and said he refused to be turned into an 'NVQ freak'. The handbook will provide some guidance through the emerging issues and terminology.

It has been written at a time of significant developments in thinking from government level down. Much of the early work on S/NVQs was at NVQ Levels 1, 2 and 3 where roles tend to be more precisely defined and narrower than at the higher levels, and activities tend to be more routine. It is comparatively easy to relate these NVQ levels to what people do at the workplace and to establish standards of performance that reflect the needs of both employer and indidividual. This relationship becomes more complex with managerial and professional activities which can vary considerably in different contexts and for which the measurement of observable outcomes undertaken at the workplace is only one indicator of capability. Thus, now that more and more higher level NVQs are coming on stream, the very structure of NVQs is being revisited and re-evaluated. What is the role of knowledge and understanding compared to lower level awards? Should it be specified in a different way than heretofore? Should cognitive skills be specified? What about values and ethics? It must be remembered that NVQs are very new and higher level NVQs even newer. It is to be expected that new approaches will be developed as experience is gained by providers and awarding bodies.

The handbook has a strong focus on assessment issues – inevitably, since S/NVQs are designed to be assessment-driven qualifications. Many NVQ assessment centres and assessors started life dealing with candidates for lower level NVQ awards and have little experience of higher level qualifications. For higher levels the nature of assessment changes. It is increasingly more difficult – and less relevant – to carry out direct observation of what an individual does at the workplace as one progresses up the NVQ levels. For example, workplace activities at the lower levels tend to be more time-bound. In other words there is a predictable amount of time from the start of an activity to its completion. This is much less often the case at higher levels.

However, much of the assessment methodology has emanated from experiences generated at the lower levels. Level 4 qualification structures are still comparatively rare and, outside of the management arena, level 5 qualifications scarcely exist. Indeed, the original NVQ framework only consisted of four levels and the first level 5 descriptor introduced in 1990 only stated 'competence in all professional areas above level 4'.

This handbook is designed to be a guide through issues and practices associated with providing and assessing higher level S/NVQs. In so doing it addresses a number of other issues such as:

- Their relationship to higher level awards offered by the university sector and how universities might respond to S/NVQ thinking.
- Their take-up by professional bodies and whether they will replace or run alongside syllabus-based awards.

Thus the development of higher level S/NVQs leads to the question of whether they should replace or supplement professional qualifications and professionally oriented qualifications offered by further and higher education institutions, including universities.

Candidates as well as centres need clear guidance over the relationship between different qualification structures, their professional standing, and how one can progress as a learner between and across the systems. This handbook will identify possible relationships, recognizing that developing these will require a positive attitude amongst the various participants. A recent Employment Department funded project in the Training & Development area in which I was involved showed considerable goodwill amongst respondents to establish clear relationships between the professionally oriented qualifications offered by Higher Education Institutions and higher level NVQs

This handbook will try to avoid getting involved in a theoretical argument over the value or otherwise of NVQs, and try not to present what has sometimes been referred to as an 'impoverished' view of NVQs. It will contend that they possess the flexibility to respond to the needs of learners, employers and professional bodies alike. Much talk has been made of reducing the emphasis on work-placed assessment and permitting far more evidence from simulations, role playing, etc. My view is that what gives NVQs their distinctive characteristics are the opportunities they afford for learning to be grounded in evidence based on 'hands-on' experiences, bearing in mind that the notion of the workplace itself is undergoing a transformation as, increasingly, people operate from home or are in constant transit from one location to another.

Each section of the handbook is intended to address specific areas of interest. The first section provides a general outline of current issues relating to the positioning of higher level NVQs within the national qualification system. The second section looks specifically at issues for providers of higher level NVQs – who might also be providers of qualifications for non-NVQ awarding bodies. It also looks at areas of concern for current and would-be assessors and verifiers of higher level NVQs. Wherever possible, guidelines and approaches are drawn from both my personal experience as an assessor/verifier/provider as well as the experiences of others operating in the field, many of whom have been developing responses to previously unaddressed problems which have emerged as they introduced new programmes and responded to candidates' needs.

Reference

1   Fletcher S. (1991) *NVQ Standards and Competence*, Kogan Page.

Acknowledgements

This has not been an easy book to write as new ways of thinking about higher level NVQs were constantly emerging. I would like to thank my publisher, Jonathan Glasspool, for his patience while I tried to explain yet another change to the system which enforced yet another delay. I would also like to thank those fellow members of the qualification cross-mapping project which is referred to a number of times in the text – in particular Sally Sambrook, the research officer, and Alan Moon who kept it on track. This piece of research provided a range of very helpful insights into the NVQ system in practice.

Finally, I would like to thank my wife, Sue, for her forbearance while I dominated the word processor at a time when she was trying to work on her own book of poems.

Part One

NVQs and Higher Education: The Practical Implications

1 Introduction to NVQs

Objectives

By the end of this general introduction you should be able to:

1 Describe the basic features of NVQs and the principles underpinning them.
2 Differentiate between NVQ levels.
3 Describe what is meant by an 'NVQ standard'.

What is an NVQ

The definition of an NVQ and the philosophy behind it seem, on the surface, to be very straightforward. Appearances, however, can be deceptive.

An NVQ is defined as:

a statement of competence clearly relevant to work and intended to facilitate entry into or progression in employment and further learning issued to an individual by a recognized awarding body.

The statement should incorporate specified standards in:

- The ability to perform in a range of work-related activities.
- The underpinning skills, knowledge and understanding required for performance in employment.

(From *NVQ Criteria and Procedures*, NCVQ, 1989 (1).)

The National Council for Vocational Qualifications (NCVQ) was set up by the Government in 1986, and was asked to 'hallmark' such qualifications which met the needs of employment and to locate them within a new structure which everyone could use and understand – the NVQ Framework.

The S/NVQ system is based on five levels, each reflecting increasingly complex occupational roles. Qualifications can be obtained at each level. The early work on developing S/NVQs was done at the lower levels. The type of activity within these lower levels can be predicated from the level descriptors (see Figure 1.1). Contrast the statements for

Level 1	Competence in the performance of work activities which are in the main routine and predictable or provide a broad foundation, primarily as a basis for progression.
Level 2	Competence in a broader and more demanding range of work activities involving greater individual responsibility and autonomy than at level 1.
Level 3	Competence in skilled areas that involve performance of a broad range of work activities, including many that are complex and non-routine. In some areas, supervisory competence may be a requirement at this level.
Level 4	Competence in a broad range of complex, technical or professional work activities performed in a wide variety of contexts and with a substantial degree of personal responsibility and autonomy. Responsibility for the work of others and the allocation of resources is often present.
Level 5	Competence which involves the application of a significant range of fundamental principles and complex techniques across a wide range of contexts. Very substantial personal autonomy and often significant responsibility for the work of others and for the allocation of substantial resources feature strongly, as do personal accountabilities for the analysis and diagnosis, design, planning, execution and evaluation.

Figure 1.1 Descriptors for NVQ levels 1–5

levels 1–3 with the level descriptors for levels 4 and 5 – in particular, compare those for levels 1 and 2 with those for levels 4 and 5. It would be highly unlikely to expect that the same methods and requirements of assessment could be applied to descriptors which are so fundamentally dissimilar. The issue of assessment at the higher levels will be addressed throughout the handbook.

S/NVQs follow a common format and structure (see Figure 1.2). The NVQ structure has become increasingly complex as it has developed

- The **title** of the NVQ
- The **units** of competence which make up the **award**
- The **elements of competence** making up each unit
- The **performance criteria** which make up each element of competence
- The **range statements** attached to each element of competence
- The **knowledge specifications** attached to each element of competence
- The **evidence requirements** attached to each element of competence

Figure 1.2 Format and structure of S/NVQs

over the years – the latest ingredient, introduced in 1994, has been the requirement to incorporate a separate knowledge specification for each element of competence.

Standards

The term 'standard' has two connotations in the NVQ literature. On the one hand, the word is used to indicate a level (or standard) of candidate work-based performance called 'competence', which is sufficient to justify an NVQ award. Where this standard is pitched has led to some interesting debate. Some have argued that the level is akin to a 'threshold' competence such as one reaches on passing a driving test. Extending the analogy, others have argued strongly that it is the level of performance one would expect an experienced driver to demonstrate (hopefully on a day that he or she is not suffering from road rage!). The spirit of the qualification is that the standard should be set closer to that of someone who is 'experienced' as opposed to 'just qualified'. But it is by no means clear-cut.

On the other hand, the term 'standard' can also be used to refer to the set of written, predetermined criteria comprising the elements of competence. These 'standards' are the 'occupational standards' which make up the NVQ units. They are precise, agreed and nationally applicable descriptions of what people in particular occupations are expected to be able to do. Competence in each part of these 'standards' needs to be fully demonstrated by a candidate. The evidence requirements indicate the types of evidence that should be drawn upon.

The 'standards' are referred to as 'national standards'. To be accredited as an NVQ, a qualification must be:

- Based on national standards required for performance in employment, and take proper account of future needs with regard to technology, markets and employment patterns.
- Awarded on the basis of valid and reliable assessments made in such a way as to ensure that performance to the national standard can be achieved at work.

(*Guide to National Vocational Qualifications*, NCVQ, March 1991 (2).)

The reasoning behind the 'national standard' model is to quality-assure the qualification for employers. Wherever an NVQ is taken the assessment level should be the same, and the arena in which competence has been demonstrated identical. Employers can thus be confident of both the level and coverage of an NVQ award. Possessors of an NVQ can be confident that it has 'transfer value' within a given employment sector. To quality-assure the qualification further, a network

of accredited assessors and verifiers for each occupational area is bein
established. This is addressed in some detail in subsequent sections.

It is the responsibility of *lead bodies* to define, maintain and improv
the standards for a given occupational area. In other words it is the re
sponsibility of each lead body to ensure that appropriate elements c
competence are written for their occupational area. Lead bodies didn
exist, as such, before the introduction of NVQs. Now there are a cor
siderable number, each representing a discrete sector of employment. I
is a requirement that they are recognized by the Employment and Edu
cation Department. To achieve this recognition each lead body mus
have credibility as broad-based, employer-led organizations. The lea
body for the broad area of management is the National Forum fc
Management Education and Development (NFMED). Its executive arr
is the Management Charter Initiative (MCI).

Each candidate needs to be provided with a set of the standard
making up an award. Assuming 10 units, each consisting of 3 element:
that is a minimum of 30 pages. As the standards get more complex an
detailed, the number of pages can be doubled. The MCI II assessmer
guidance consists of 92 pages.

The NCVQ is conscious of this. The 1995 *NVQ Criteria and Guidanc*
(3) states:

NCVQ encourages the listing of performance criteria, range statemen
knowledge specification and evidence requirements for each elemer
together, where possible, on a single page. In any event elements an
their performance criteria should not be shown on different non-facin
pages.

It is a requirement that the standards are *transparent*, i.e. it is mad
clear to the candidates exactly what is expected of them and the criteri
against which they are to be assessed. However, the requirement fo
transparency creates a dilemma. How can a form of words be foun
which compresses element statements and performance criteria, so tha
they don't become too extensive, and still makes them intelligible an
meaningful to assessors and candidates alike.

Despite the requirement for transparency, the need to compress th
standards into a meaningful package means that considerable amount
of time are spent with candidates explaining to them precisely what th
standards mean. It is not just a matter of linguistics. Invariably
number of people will have been involved, if not in their writing, i
their approval, and each may well have a different perspective on wha
the standards in a particular occupational area should consist of. Thi
need to accommodate a number of viewpoints can be at the expense c
clarity and coherence unless great care is exercised by the lead body.

Confirmed NVQ addicts and afficionados make much of the distinc
tion between 'competences' and 'competencies'. The correct term t

use is 'competences'. 'Competencies' are held to refer to the personal qualities that one brings to the workplace, not the outcomes of one's work activity which are captured by the term 'competences'. The focus of the NVQ rubric has always been on its outcome-driven characteristics.

Components of an NVQ

The 1995 *NVQ Criteria and Guidance* (3) provide more detailed information on the various components of an NVQ and the following analysis is based on this publication.

Title

The use of words such as 'certificate' or 'diploma' is not permissible for an NVQ qualification, although the award of an NVQ will naturally result in a certificate. So if a candidate asks you whether they will get a certificate the answer will be 'Yes, but it won't be called one!'. The award title should be sufficiently explicit to communicate clearly the area of competence and should also indicate the level.

The title 'NVQ Certificate in Management' is not permissible, but NVQ level 4 in Management' would be. The Guide gives no explanation as to why the words 'certificate' and 'diploma' are taboo.

Units

Units are the lowest level at which accreditation can be given. A number of units make up the full qualification, but it is possible to gain individual unit accreditation. Each unit should make approximately equal demands on a candidate in terms of the competences contained and the knowledge and skills necessary. Each unit must also have a title. If a unit's title is sufficiently clear, explanatory information is not required. However, a unit commentary is often provided to supplement the title, and describe the unit's relationship to other units. For a full NVQ the range of units would normally be between 5 and 15.

Elements of competence

An element of competence (often shortened in NVQ parlance to an 'element') is what people usually mean when they refer to an NVQ standard. Each element consists of four items (see Figure 1.3).

The element title describes what a person should be able to do at work and should be expressed in language which makes sense to the

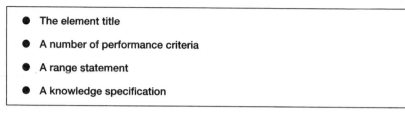

Figure 1.3   The structure of an element

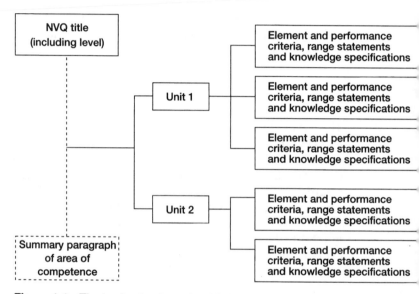

Figure 1.4   The basic structure of an NVQ

people who will use it. The other parts of the standard should always be read in the context of the title, and not taken in isolation.

Most of the work done by candidates and assessors with NVQ standards will be at element level. Candidates will be concerned with interpreting the elements and producing evidence that will demonstrate their competence. Assessors will be judging whether the evidence is sufficient and suitable.

A number of elements, typically 3 or 4, make up a unit.

Performance criteria

Performance criteria must accompany each element of competence. They describe *critical outcomes* of successful performance, and must contain *evaluative statements* which define the acceptable level of performance required in employment.

Thus if we look at one of the performance criteria for an element within the National Standards for Assessment and Verification developed by the Training and Development Lead Body (TDLB).

- *Element title*: Verify assessment practice
- *Performance criterion*: (a) The eligibility of individuals to practise as assessors is checked against awarding body criteria.
- *Critical outcome*: The eligibility of individuals to practise as assessors.
- *Evaluative statement*: Is checked against awarding body criteria.

Exercise. Take the rest of the performance criteria for this element and try to differentiate between critical outcomes and evaluative statements. Does it work each time?

(b) Assessment practice and quality assurance arrangements are monitored in an appropriate proportion of instances to check that they meet awarding body requirements.

(c) Assessors are given clear and constructive feedback.

(d) Judgments of evidence and assessment decisions are sampled regularly against the national standards to check their fairness and accuracy.

(e) Documentation is complete, accurate and up to date.

(f) Decision-makers are given clear explanations of the need for improvements in assessment practice.

(g) Disputes and appeals are referred to the appropriate authority.

(h) Recommendations for awarding body action to maintain the quality of assessment are presented clearly and promptly to the external verifier

ange statements

A range statement is also part of each element. It should specify the various circumstances or contexts in which the performance criteria are to be applied. Areas covered could include key differences in physical location, employment contexts and equipment used.

These might be specified as follows:

- *Physical location*: factory; office.
- *Employment contexts*: full-time; part-time; self-employed subcontractor
- *Equipment used*: Telephone; fax; photocopier

Whatever is specified must clearly relate, in a way that is comprehensible to the candidate and assessor, to the performance criteria for the element in question.

Knowledge specifications

These are a recent addition to the NVQ rubric. They are not as such par
of the statement of competence in the sense that competence is a dem
onstration of what you can do and not what you know. Nevertheless
they need to be attached and contextualized to each element. As w
shall see, this ruling can be unduly restrictive and make it difficult t
capture the breadth of knowledge that might be associated with
given occupational area. Because of their comparative newness, there i
not much experience of writing knowledge specifications.

Evidence requirements

Evidence requirements must also be provided for each element by th
lead body. They must state the minimum performance evidenc
acceptable. Performance evidence covers two categories: workplac
evidence and simulations.

Workplace evidence

The NCVQ guidelines for NVQ assessment have always emphasize
the primacy of performance evidence as demonstrated by means c
work-placed assessment. For example, the 1991 Guide states that:

... performance must be demonstrated and assessed under condition
as close as possible to those under which it would normally be practise
– preferably in the workplace. (2: p. 6)

In today's environment it is difficult to establish what the workplac
is for many people. Many aspects of creative work are done from hom
Reports are often written from home. Is preparatory work on a train c
on a plane 'the workplace'? A number of organizations are er
couraging staff to work from home. Feedback surveys by companie
such as Digital, Rank Xerox and Mercury show that being able to spen
a proportion of time at home, with portable kit so as to stay in touc
with the office is considered immensely beneficial. As Stephen Jupr
head of flexible working at Digital has commented, 'Home is perceive
as a quality environment: it is where people feel they are at their mos
productive'.

The lower level NVQs deal with candidates who are often engage
in time-bound activities, which are observable as they are being don
and which are undertaken at a particular place.

The guidelines go on to state that:

... if assessment in the workplace is not practicable, simulations, tests, projects or assignments may provide suitable evidence – but care must be taken to ensure that all elements and performance criteria have been covered, and that it is possible to predict that the competence assessed can be sustained in performance.

Simulations are often considered to be opportunities to test individuals in activities which are not demonstrable at the workplace. This is often because they deal with contingencies that hopefully will not happen, such as dealing with an emergency. They are also often used to provide opportunities for people who are unemployed, between jobs, or for other reasons cannot demonstrate workplace evidence. Discussions have taken place as to how much of NVQ assessment should be based on simulations without taking away the distinctive work-based performance focus which is the rationale for the qualification. Should it be no more than 20 per cent? or 50 per cent? or some other figure? No definitive figure has ever been provided.

Some hard-line exponents of the S/NVQ ethos have emphasized the 'primacy of naturally occurring evidence from the workplace' and argued that anything else is, in essence, a 'simulation'. 'Naturally occurring' relates to experiences which occur as part of day-to-day operations without any artificial intervention or activities designed to meet the needs of assessment. This view seems to me to be based on a misapprehension of what the workplace is all about. In terms of personal development strategies, it has been commonplace for years for individuals to be provided with developmental opportunities which transcend their day-to-day role. How otherwise do people develop? How do employers help ensure that their staff have the skills to cope with the challenges of future job roles.

Supplementary evidence

Evidence requirements also consist of *knowledge and understanding*

Knowledge and understanding have always been seen as secondary to, and underpinning of, performance, rather than having value in their own right. Figure 1.5 taken from the 1991 Guide groups knowledge, principles, theory and cognitive skills together. They are shown as sources of supplementary evidence for inferring that a candidate has competence in an element.

The place and assessment of knowledge and understanding has come to the fore as an issue with the development of higher level NVQs. There is an increasing recognition that they are not underpinning and

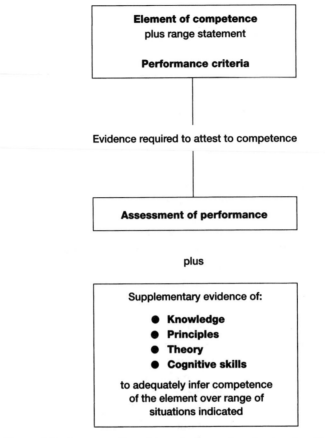

Figure 1.5 Incorporation of knowledge and understanding (From *Guide to National Vocational Qualifications*, NCVQ, March 1991, p. 16)

that their demonstration is not necessarily subordinate to performance. The February 1995 'vision' document published by the Employment Department (4) makes the following statement:

> Knowledge is an integral part of competence at all levels of occupation and, in NVQs and SVQs it must be demonstrable through assessment. At lower levels much of it can be inferred in the process of assessment; at higher levels of occupation however, mastery and exploitation of bodies and patterns of knowledge, of concepts and paradigms, of precedent and process is vital for satisfactory performance.

Implicit in this statement is the need to operate with different assessment strategies to those adopted for the lower level NVQs.

This is taken forward in the document.

The development of higher level vocational qualifications will require further work to explore approaches to assessment which are capable of capturing the complexities of occupational roles at this level, for example high levels of personal responsibility, unpredictable nature of problems and a capacity for self improvement and evaluation. (4: p. 8)

An interesting recent development has been an attempt to redefine competence so as to emphasize even further the role of knowledge and understanding. The October 1995 Consultation Document (5) produced by the Evaluation Advisory Group established by the Government to review the 100 most used NVQs defines competence as:

The ability to apply knowledge and understanding in performing to the standards required in employment, including solving problems and meeting changing demands. (5: p. 4)

Perhaps this is a definition one might expect from a group that has as one of its members Professor Alan Smithers, Director of the Centre for Education and Employment Research at the University of Manchester. Professor Smithers has been for some time forcefully and publically critical of NVQs as developed and assessed to date. It is, however, a definition, which could equally be applied to many vocationally oriented qualifications

Assessment and verification

Assessment is an issue in any qualification structure. One of the distinctive characteristics of the NVQ system is the need for those individuals carrying out assessment activities to be accredited as assessors. The implications of this for higher level NVQs is specifically addressed in this book. Similarly, those individuals responsible for managing the NVQ process need to be accredited both as assessors and as verifiers. In other words people need to get what are known as the TDLB D units. These were produced by the Training and Development Lead Body because it was felt that trainers would know what assessment was all about. They were called the D Units to reflect the training cycle.

- *A Units* are concerned with the identification of training needs.
- *B Units* are concerned with the design of training strategies and programmes to meet those needs.
- *C Units* are concerned with the delivery of training programmes to meet the needs.
- *D Units* are concerned with assessment and evaluation.

Conclusion

Over the relatively short period of time I have been preparing this book there have been significant changes in the NVQ rubric. In particular there has been increasing emphasis on knowledge and understanding. The implications of these changes have, in my opinion, not yet fully filtered through to provider level. And there could be more on the way depending on the national responses to the Review of 100 NVQs, SVQs and the subsequent Beaumont report. I shall end this section by leaving you with a few of the questions that were asked, for you to reflect upon.

- Are competence-based standards the right basis for framing vocational qualifications to meet the needs of employment?
- To what extent does the competence-based approach to qualifications provide scope for the development of learning programmes?
- How suitable are NVQs/SVQs as qualifications for those preparing to enter employment as well as those who are already in work?
- What do you think of the way that knowledge and understanding is expressed in the standards with which you are familiar?
- To what extent should assessment of knowledge and understanding be fully integrated with the assessment of performance?
- Should knowledge and understanding be specified and/or assessed differently for NVQs/SVQs ar different levels of the framework? If yes please suggest what those differences might be? [This is a crucial question for this handbook!]
- To what extent does the current NVQ/SVQ assessment process guarantee the occupational competence of successful candidates?
- How appropriately is simulation being used within NVQs/SVQs? For example, is reluctance to use simulation resulting in excessive costs or is too frequent use of simulation undermining the validity of the qualification in employment?
- What encourages or discourages take-up of NVQs/SVQs in particular sectors? How can any problems of access for individuals be overcome?

References

1 *NVQ Criteria and Guidance*, NCVQ, 1989.
2 *Guide to National Vocational Qualifications*, NCVQ, March 1991.
3 *NVQ Criteria and Guidance*, NCVQ, January 1995.
4 *A Vision for Higher Level Qualifications*, Employment Department, February 1995.
5 Consultation Document, Evaluation Advisory Group, October 1995.

2 The impact of NVQs on higher level vocational qualifications

Objectives

By the end of this chapter you should be able to:

1 Identify the various components of the emerging education structure.
2 Establish the potential impact of higher level NVQs on traditional qualifications.
3 Describe different responses of professional bodies and education institutions to NVQs.

Introduction

The period since 1986 has seen the emergence of two additional, albeit related, vocational qualification systems in the UK as the result of Government intervention. 1986 saw the introduction of NVQs and 1991 saw the emergence of GNVQs.

As we have seen, NVQs have five levels. Levels 4 and 5 are intended to cover the upper echelons of occupational areas. As NVQs at these levels come on stream, they are competing in the same marketplace as existing professional qualifications and occupationally specific post-graduate qualifications. The 'national standards' that make up each NVQ similarly may be seen to compete with existing 'professional standards'.

GNVQs currently have three levels, although the expectation is that five levels will be in place over the next few years. At the time of writing, their impact on higher level qualifications is minimal, although this situation could change rapidly.

The main focus of this section is the impact of higher level NVQs on conventional, occupationally specific, higher level qualifications of the sort that were in place before NVQs were developed. These include:

- Qualifications offered independently, or through designated centres, by professional bodies, often leading to enhanced professional membership status.
- Post-graduate level (as opposed to first degree level), qualifications offered by universities, often linked to professional body qualifications.

As more and more higher level NVQ qualifications have been introduced, there have been a series of attempts to modify the traditional academic rubric to address the problems and challenges posed by students needing to demonstrate relevant work-related performance.

Another linked development has been the emergence of a variety of arrangements by university and other centres to offer 'pick and mix' programmes for candidates, to take into account their needs and opportunities. Not all candidates have work roles that allow them to generate the evidence required for an NVQ. Not all employers are supportive. How does one deal with unemployed candidates or those looking for a career shift? Some candidates prefer the structured learning processes associated with 'academic' programmes which specifically analyse and often challenge the body of knowledge and theories and paradigms associated with an occupational area.

Both professional bodies and universities and other higher education institutions are having to consider their attitude to higher level NVQs. They can choose:

- To ignore them and hope they will go away.
- To disparage them and hope they will go away.
- To welcome them and encourage their development.
- To wait and see.
- To impose conditions on their acceptibility.
- To offer them in addition to (or as an alternative to) existing qualifications.
- To offer them as a replacement to existing qualifications.
- To see them as equivalents to existing qualifications and afford them parity of esteem.
- To see them as lesser than existing qualifications.
- To see them as better than existing qualifications.

All of the above perspectives have been, and continue to be, expressed.

It is difficult to ignore them given the Government's drive for their introduction. The National Educational and Training Targets announced by the National Training Task Force in 1992 were that, by 1996, 50 per cent of the workforce should be aiming for NVQs or units towards them. The Foreword to the March 1991 *Guide to National Vocational Qualifications* (1) referred to the NCVQ target of having qualifications in place at Levels 1 to 4 covering 80 per cent of the working population by the end of 1992.

A unified vocational qualification system or co-existence?

Many considered that the Government's original hope was to have a unified vocational qualification system in the UK, based on national occupational standards with clearly defined progression routes for candidates. Thus in the early 1990s there was a feeling abroad in some quarters that ultimately NVQs (and associated GNVQs) would come to replace the jungle of existing professional and other vocational qualifications. 'Unreformed' vocational qualifications would no longer exist.

There are still some publications coming from the public sector which adopt this perspective and argue against co-existence. For example, the June 1995 *GNVQ Briefing* document from NCVQ (2) states in the Introduction that:

> . . . the Government intends that GNVQs, together with National Vocational Qualifications (NVQs), will replace other vocational qualifications and become the main national provision for vocational education and training.

A number of recent formulations project a less ambitious perspective. A December 1994 letter from the Secretary of State for Employment to the Chairman of the NCVQ, setting out ministerial priorities for the NCVQ stated:

> Government still anticipates, in due course, a progressive structure of NVQs (and SVQs) covering all occupations at all levels.

A March 1994 letter from the same source to the Chairman of NCVQ, referring to the formation of a Higher Level Strategy Group stated:

> It will be important for NCVQ (and SCOTVEC for Scottish GSVQ/SVQ interests) to consider in due course how GNVQs and NVQs can fit together coherently with academic and professional qualifications, to ensure effective progression to full occupational competence at work, which takes full account of the interests of Higher Education.

The Higher Level Strategy Group produced *A Vision for Higher Level Qualifications* in February 1995 (3). The tone and comments have clearly moved away from the notion of a 'unified' vocational qualification structure:

> The prime objective, in terms of vocational qualification, is to extend the current provision and to provide a comprehensive framework embracing levels 4 and 5. Progressive pathways to the highest levels would be generated in all occupational sectors, including both occupational NVQs/SVQs and the emerging general vocational qualifications.

The vision however extends beyond that. It involves a clarification of the relationships between NVQs/SVQs, awards offered by statutory and professional bodies and higher education. No single qualification pattern will satisfy the needs of the many and varied higher level sectors of employment. In most areas it is likely that different kinds of qualification (vocational and academic) would coexist, each serving its own particular purpose.

Nevertheless, the aim is to obtain a consensus on the nature of qualifications appropriate for different sectors and on the relationships between them. (3: p. 4)

The emphasis would seem now to be not on replacing qualifications but on introducing new, competence-based qualifications at the higher levels which reinforce existing programmes.

Thus for the foreseeable future there will be three parallel vocational systems co-existing, and perhaps meeting, different employment needs. These three systems are:

- The NVQ (SVQ).
- The GNVQ (SNVQ).
- 'Traditional educational', which covers non-NVQ qualifications offered by universities/colleges/examining bodies/professional bodies and grouped together as a sort of amorphous mass.

Work has been done recently to challenge the homogeneous way of perceiving the 'academic' world. For example, Atkins et al. (4) have suggested that there are likely to be four main purposes of higher education over the next 10 years:

- A general educational experience of intrinsic worth to the individual student in its own right.
- A preparation for knowledge creation (or dissemination or application) in a particular subject or field.
- Specific vocational preparation usually linked to entry to a profession.
- Preparation for general employment not tied to any one profession, service industry, or occupational family.

While recognizing, like Atkins et al., that the balance between purposes may change from occupational area to occupational area, this handbook will focus on the relationship between NVQs and specific vocational preparation. The formulation by Atkins et al. of this category seems a trifle narrow and I feel more comfortable with 'specific vocational preparation and development'. Candidates for NVQs and students on higher education vocationally oriented courses are often already operating within an occupational area and are seeking a toolkit for their current job, and appropriate skills and understanding to equip them to progress.

Establishing relationships between qualifications

Given the likelihood of three parallel but distinct qualification systems being in existence, it becomes important to establish how they relate to each other.

Students and candidates will wish to know how a qualification in one system relates to another in terms of progression. Questions will include:

- If I have an NVQ level 4 or 5, will this entitle me to professional membership?
- If I have an NVQ level 5, will this give me exemptions from a related post-graduate diploma or master's qualification?
- If I have an NVQ level 5, is this post-graduate level? Is it better, worse or broadly equivalent?
- If I have a post-graduate certificate/diploma/masters qualification, will this entitle me to an NVQ level 5? If not, what will I have to do?

Responses to NVQs

Professional bodies and accrediting bodies (such as BTEC) will need to form a judgement:

- Do we replace our traditional higher level qualifications with NVQ levels 4 and/or 5?
- Do we offer extra qualifications? If so, how do they relate to each other?
- Do we offer 'hybrid' qualifications, with both traditional and NVQ elements?

BTEC's position is that it is committed to the development of NVQs and GNVQs within the national framework, and 'in a strong position to contributing effectively . . . to ensuring parity of esteem with academic qualifications at the same level through national standards against which achievement in work-related education will be judged' (5).

The Institute of Management (IM) has developed its Competent Manager Programme, providing opportunities for candidates to obtain NVQs at levels 4 and 5, using Management Charter Initiative (MCI) standards. However, their position is that the traditional route to management qualifications is likely to maintain its current popularity and that individuals should be provided with free access to academic and vocational qualification frameworks.

Universities will need to address the above questions now that the Department of Education and the relevant arm of the Department of Employment have merged (as of July 1995). It will be increasingly difficult to evade the issue. The Committee of Vice Chancellors and Principals (CVCP) in September 1994 made a statement in which it agreed to support the involvement of universities in the development of higher level S/NVQs and in the possible future development of higher level GNVQs/GSVQs. The Chairman of the CVCP additionally said that:

Universities support the development of competence based approaches provided that they integrate and develop the cognitive, core and subject-specific abilities to levels which are comparable with those already attained in existing HE programmes of vocational education. (6)

A number of universities are already involved in S/NVQ work. A survey conducted by the CVCP in 1994 demonstrated considerable interest and both current and future potential involvement in the NVQ qualification system. Out of a possible 123, 74 responded to a CVCP questionnaire, and of the responders 18 (24 per cent) were already offering courses leading to the award of an S/NVQ at level 4 or 5 and a further 16 (22 per cent) were planning to offer courses leading to a level 4 or 5 award. Interestingly, 4 (5 per cent) institutions had made a policy decision not to offer S/NVQs, 18 (24 per cent) had yet to consider the issue, and 18 (24 per cent) were considering the issue but had not yet reached a decision (6).

The Open University is currently the only university which is an approved NVQ awarding body in its own right. However, the consortium of university business schools, known as the Association of Business Schools (ABS), has created the Management Verification Consortium (MVC). This is an approved NVQ awarding body for those of its member institutions who wish to offer NVQs, particularly in the management area.

Many universities work in partnership with professional institutions in offering programmes which lead to awards recognized by the professional body concerned. Examples include law, medicine, engineering, management, personnel, training and development. Many students choose universities which offer them the opportunity of a qualification with a profession member status attached to it. NVQ standards at the higher levels are being developed across the range of the professional bodies' spheres of activity. The standards are developed by employer-led lead bodies, which are independent of particular professional bodies whilst being fully represented on them.

However, the universities are often 'tied' in terms of their market to the professional bodies and are likely to adjust their post-experience/post-graduate qualifications in line with professional requirements. Thus, if a professional body decides to bring all its qualifications in line with the lead body NVQ occupational standards for its area, then the partner universities will probably follow.

There can, however, be tension, and some jealousy, in the relationship between lead bodies and professional bodies. Professional bodies consider themselves to be guardians of standards in their area and control entry to the various grades of professional membership. The development of standards – even those to which they have been given the opportunity to contribute – can be seen as an intrusion. There is also an implication that in the past the professions 'have got it wrong' and that their standards and qualifications 'are not meeting employer/national needs'.

It is unlikely, at present, that NVQs at higher levels will replace traditional qualifications. It is likely that, over time, traditional qualifications will adjust some of their assessment methodology and programme structure to demonstrate greater congruence with NVQ standards. Much depends on how well the NVQ standards are written.

Some past criticisms of offering NVQs as higher level qualifications

Over the last few years, as higher level NVQs have begun to come on stream, there have been some modifications to the NVQ rubric to take on board some of the difficulties and experiences that have emerged from the field. In particular, concerns have been expressed about knowledge and understanding. One of the problems is that knowledge and understanding is tied to individual elements of competence and is not domain-specific. 'Domain-specific' means the existence of certain concepts and principles which overarch the whole arena and cannot easily be contextualized to any individual standard. The bodies of knowledge associated with organizational dynamics and with motivational theory are two cases in point.

Another criticism has related to the development of cognitive skills. The units and elements of competence, it has been held, are so atomized that they do not permit the development of broad cognitive skills such as the ability to synthesize information from a variety of sources across the domain.

Yet another criticism has related to the apparent absence of ethical judgements in early standards.

Recent attempts to resolve these criticisms

The January 1995 *NVQ Criteria and Guidance* (7) has gone some way to trying to meet these criticisms; thus, in respect of knowledge and understanding it states:

The NVQ statement of competence concentrates on the ability to perform effectively. However, effective performance depends on the individual having an appropriate body of knowledge, theory, principles and cognitive skills on which to draw. While the ultimate focus of NVQs and their constituent units must be effective performance, much of the contributory learning and assessment will deal with knowledge understanding and skills. (7: pp. 16–17)

However, this statement still does not go sufficiently far to meet a academic, professional and practitioner criticisms. Thus, subsequer qualifying statements in the Guide state:

It is the responsibility of the lead body to provide specification of essen tial knowledge and understanding which should:

- only include knowledge which clearly supports the performanc detailed in the statement of competence . . .
- specifies the relevant imformation and principles in a way whic shows how they apply in performance
- relates the knowledge clearly to each element. (7: pp. 26–27)

Have the criticisms been answered?

One is still left with the feeling that knowledge and understanding i being 'atomized' and narrowed down artificially to meet the impera tive of performance. One consequence in standards-design practice ha been much repetition of the same 'chunk' of knowledge across a sprea of elements and units.

Another disappointment is the undeveloped view of cognitive skills which are grouped together as part of knowledge and understanding This is exemplified by the statement that:

'Knowledge and understanding' is used as shorthand within NVQs t cover not the body of facts and principles needed for competent per formance, but also the associated cognitive skills. (7: p. 30)

It is a gross oversimplification to see cognitive skills as akin to know ledge and understanding, and this is a source of much potential con fusion. Without going into great detail about various theories o knowledge, facts, theories and principles can be conceived of as com prising the knowledge base; what we need to know about, in order t act and interpret with confidence in our occupational area. There are number of typologies that move us from such a knowledge base. Fo example, Volet and Chalmers (8), have proposed the following 'goal positions on a continuum of learning, moving from a 'surface' knowledge to a 'deep' understanding:

- Remember key features of material presented.
- Acquire more knowledge about the theories in a subject area.

- Understand the theories.
- Critically assess the theories as they apply to the real world.
- Construct own theoretical perspectives to explain the 'real world' in the field of study.

The cognitive skills are the processes of obtaining these various 'goal' positions.

This formulation has echoes of the well known Bloom (9) 'cognitive domain hierarchy', which differentiates between five types of learning, progressing up through a higher order:

- *Knowledge* refers to the ability to recall or recognize facts, rules or concepts.
- *Comprehension* refers to the ability to understand facts and concepts.
- *Application* refers to the ability to use facts and concepts to solve new problems.
- *Synthesis* refers to the ability to integrate components into a new cycle.
- *Evaluation* refers to the ability to judge and compare procedures, products, etc.

Kaufman (10) develops the relationship between a knowledge base and cognitive skills. In reviewing a range of studies that relate knowledge and understanding to expert performance, he suggests that:

The results of research on expertise seem to show that the possession of extensive, well-organized, 'domain-specific' knowledge is a crucial factor in expert performance. The point here is not only the rather trivial one that experts out-perform novices because they have more factual information about the task. Rather, the important point is that a higher level of organized, 'domain-specific' knowledge gives the expert access to more powerful problem-solving methods. Thus, high level cognitive abilities should not be seen as existing apart from knowledge. Rather, powerful cognitive operations seem only to materialize in a system of well-organized extensive knowledge. (10)

The separation of cognitive skills from knowledge and understanding has long been a feature of 'traditional' higher level vocational awards – indeed of most 'academic' qualifications. The general educational objectives of the former Council for National Academic Awards (CNAA) (11), which oversaw polytechnic academic standards included the development of students':

- Intellectual and imaginative powers.
- Understanding and judgement.
- Problem-solving skills.

- Ability to see relationships within what they have learned and to perceive their field of study in a broader perspective.

Other typical criteria are those listed by Walton (12) and now followed by the University of Sunderland:

In order to achieve Masters credits, and therefore be accredited with the University of Sunderland Post-graduate Certificate as well as an NVQ level 4, candidates need to bring forward evidence that they have the skills, abilities and attitudes which are not necessarily apparent in the evidence generated for their portfolio.
Candidates will be expected to demonstrate the ability to

- argue rationally and draw independent conclusions based on a rigorous, analytical and critical approach to data, demonstration and argument
- reflect the interrelationship between theory and practice
- demonstrate some originality and reflection
- demonstrate the capacity for initiating change in response to earlier reflections.

In the recent Employment Department *Qualifications Mapping Project – Training and Development S/NVQs and Academic Qualifications* (13) the following set of criteria were developed for credit rating NVQs at post-graduate level:

---

1   The ability to reflect critically on the totality of an occupationally relevant group of competencies in the light of knowledge of the field and practitioner experience.
2   The ability to relate critical reflections to existing comprehensive conceptual frameworks and generate new frameworks should existing frameworks not be adequate.
3   The ability to relate critical reflections and conceptual constructs to practical professional situations at an appropriate level, and through analysis to determine sound courses of action.
4   The ability to present, and to argue logically, proposals for courses of action based on models of good practice.
5   The possession of a body of knowledge and conceptual frameworks of sufficient breadth and depth to be confident that reflections, proposals and actions are adequately grounded.

The report argues that the first four criteria are generic cognitive skills. They are general criteria applicable across professions, and should not be attributed to individual standards. The fifth criterion represents knowledge, including that of conceptual frameworks which would be specific to each occupational area.

One of the recommendations of the report is that 'the S/NVQ definitions of level should be amplified to incorporate a statement on the generic cognitive skills required'. It remains to be seen whether this is taken up.

Ethical precepts

The 1995 *NVQ Criteria and Guidance* (7) also dealt with concerns over the incorporation of values in given occupational areas:

The statement of competence should also seek to capture all the various occupational demands which may be identified under terms such as creativity, ethics and values. This involves making explicit the characteristics of effective performance which are subsumed by broad terms such as these and capturing them within the NVQ format. (7: p. 17)

How this will be achieved in practice remains to be seen. It is not at all clear that 'creativity, ethics and values' should only be associated with individual standards. Ethics and values would seem to relate to overarching ways of behaving and represent attitudes of mind. John (14) has listed some of the most frequently mentioned examples of actions which employers generally regard as unethical:

- Giving gifts or gratuities to buyers in the hope of influencing them.
- Dishonesty towards customers and clients.
- Theft of any kind.
- 'Slagging off' the organization either internally or externally.
- Stealing someone else's ideas without giving them credit.
- Reading other people's mail for personal advantage.
- Dismissing someone without a full, impartial investigation.
- Insider trading.
- Giving rewards to certain individuals and withholding rewards from others, for reasons unconnected with performance.

Such attitudes are, of course, reflected in performance and some could quite readily be attributable to individual standards. For others this would be extremely difficult. The issue of how competence would be assessed also gives food for thought.

Conclusion

As the NVQ rubric twists and turns and bends to incorporate the external demands put on it, and yet still stay within the original disaggregated unit and element format, one has a suspicion that the standards run the risk of becoming overloaded as 'transparent', understandable and manageable statements of competence. As Alison Wolf said in a 1994 CEDEFOP article (15):

The original architects of NVQs assumed that knowledge requirements would be clearly understood by trainers and teachers on the basis of the criteria of competence. This proved optimistic. Workshops which tried to 'extract' or 'induce' knowledge requirements from standards demonstrated quite quickly that the knowledge extract was not, in fact, at all standard, but subject to very different interpretations. Formal knowledge lists followed. Finally the transparancy of assessment requirements came into question in its turn. Just as range and knowledge statements have been added to standards, so too have assessment requirements. Industry bodies are now expected to add lists of assessment specifications to the standards which examining and awarding bodies use.

Yet another level of detail and centralization is thus added. The resulting standards and qualifications have become huge and unwieldy documents. The apparently economical notion of competence has become exhaustively defined and constrained. In the process, it becomes increasingly undeliverable and increasingly unattractive to employers as a basis for either their own training programmes or as a way of certifying employees. It also becomes increasingly questionable as a suitable approach for a world of rapid technological change and fluid job boundaries.

The question arises as to whether too much is being asked of the standards if they are to maintain their integrity as a competence-driven, work-based qualification system. If we are going to have three separate vocational qualification systems in existence, each with their distinctive features and characteristics, is it significant that higher level NVQs don't address all the criticisms aimed at them?

References

1 *Guide to National Vocational Qualifications*, NCVQ, March 1991.
2 *GNVQ Briefing*, NCVQ, June 1995.
3 *A Vision for Higher Level Qualifications*, Employment Department, February 1995.
4 Atkins M.J., Beattie J. and Dockrell W.B. (1993) *Assessment Issues in Higher Education*, Employment Department, March.
5 *Implementing BTEC GNVQs – a Guide for Centres*, BTEC, June 1993.

6 Quoted in: *A Strategy for Vocational Higher Qualifications – CVCP* (*Competence and Assessment No. 29*), Employment Department, June 1995.
7 *NVQ Criteria and Guidance*, NCVQ, January 1995.
8 Volet S.E. and Chalmers D. (1992) Investigation of qualitative differences in university students' learning goals, based on an unfolding model of stage development, *British Journal of Educational Psychology*, **62**, 17–34.
9 Bloom B.S. (ed.) (1956) *Taxonomy of Educational Objectives*, Vol. 1, New York: McKay.
10 Kaufmann G. (1991) Problem solving and creativity, in Henry J. (ed.), *Creative Management*, Chap. 10, SAGE.
11 *CNAA Guidelines*, CNAA 1992.
12 Walton J. (1994) *Vocational Qualifications at Professional Level – Bridging the Academic/NVQ Divide* (*Competence and Assessment No. 26*), pp. 18–19, July.
13 *Qualifications Mapping Project – Training and Development S/NVQs and Academic Qualifications*, Employment Department, June 1995.
14 John T. (1995) Don't be afraid of the moral maze, *People Management*, **5 Oct.**, 32–34.
15 Wolf A. (1994) CEDEFOP.

3 The relationship between higher level NVQs, GNVQs and the emerging notion of capability

Objectives

By the end of this chapter you should be able to:

1 Describe the basic features of GNVQs and establish who they were originally targeted at.
2 Identify similarities and differences with NVQs.
3 Evaluate the case for specialist as opposed to generalist GNVQs.
4 Put forward arguments for and against the introduction of higher level GNVQs.
5 Establish the objectives of 'capability' or 'pre-competence' awards being offered by some centres.
6 Consider some implications from a provider's perspective of offering a Management GNVQ.

Introduction

Debling (1) contends that there are now three vocational qualification pathways in the UK: traditional educational, NVQ and GNVQ. Each pathway he considers leads to separate goals and should not be seen as equivalents. Each is designed differently in order to meet different objectives. This section will address the relationship between two of these strands – that between NVQs and GNVQs. It will also touch upon the possible future impact on professional bodies.

GNVQs are even more recent in origin than NVQs, their introduction emanating from the May 1991 Government White Paper entitled *Education and Training in the 21st Century* (2). Their original purpose was, in part, to provide an alternative to GCSEs and A levels and thus to be a central plank in the Government's education and training strategy for 16- to 19-year-olds. Indeed, Advanced GNVQs (level 3), are now being termed the 'vocational A level'.

Their growth has been remarkably rapid. In the academic year 1994–95, the second year in which they became generally available, one in four of those aged 17 had registered for GNVQ awards. It has been forecast that by the end of the century this figure will rise to 50 per cent (3).

Like NVQs, GNVQs are based on national standards (or specifications) which make explicit the learning outcomes. They are, however, designed to measure different kinds of achievement to NVQs. Thus, whereas NVQs are based upon 'statements of competence', GNVQs are based upon 'statements of attainment'. The award of a GNVQ does not imply that students can perform competently immediately after qualifying. Students will, however, have achieved general skills, knowledge and understanding which underpin a *range* of occupations.

Although what differentiates GNVQs from many academic qualifications is the occupational or employment base, in certain subjects such as science, art and design and information technology, this difference cannot be detected by the title alone. According to the June 1995 *GNVQ Briefing Note* (4) it is the orientation of the subject towards practical applications and employment that makes the GNVQ curriculum approach different from that of many academic qualifications. Of course some so-called 'academic' qualifications have always contained a strong vocational and practical element.

This strong vocational orientation means that work placements are a feature of most GNVQ courses. GNVQs require students to find out about employment and organizational practice in the related industrial sectors.

GNVQs currently only cover three levels, and level 3 is seen as the closest equivalent to A level for entry purposes into higher education institutions. The three levels are:

- Level 1: – Foundation.
- Level 2: – Intermediate.
- Level 3: – Advanced (the 'vocational or applied A level').

Level descriptors are not provided as they are for NVQs.

Consultation is currently taking place on the possible development of higher level GNVQs. The former Employment Department (5) produced the chart shown in Figure 3.1 suggesting how these might equate with vocationally oriented degrees/diplomas. The same chart shows GNVQ level 5 equating with post-graduate degrees; the September 1995 Consultation paper on GNVQs at higher levels states that equating it with a master's degree is one proposal under consideration. However, no work has yet been done on GNVQs at level 5 and the focus of current consultations is on level 4 (3: p. 18). (As constructed, NVQ levels 4/5 seem to be the pinnacle of any student's vocational attainment. Others might challenge this.)

It is these putative GNVQ levels (4 and 5) that are the subject of this section; however, it is worth noting that the Employment Department chart is not totally accurate, e.g. vocationally oriented diplomas can be staging posts en route to a master's qualification.

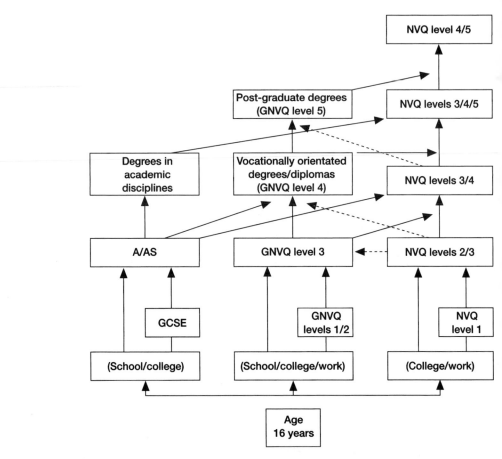

Figure 3.1 The relationship between qualification systems (From *A Strategy for Vocational Higher Education*, Employment Department, June 1995)

Features of GNVQs

GNVQs include the following features:

1. They have to consist of:

- Mandatory vocational units.
- Optional vocational units.
- Core skills units.

At advanced level it is a requirement that there are eight mandatory units, four optional units and three core skill units. The NCVQ 'owns' the mandatory vocational units and the core skills units and these units are common to all awarding bodies for a given occupational area. Individual awarding bodies are given discretion over optional units and also over any additional units they may wish to incorporate. The number of mandatory and optional units for level 4 has not yet been decided.

2. The core skills units must cover:

- communication,
- application of number,
- information technology,

irrespective of the level of award or the broad occupational area covered.

3. Like NVQs, each unit is made up of a number of elements, with performance criteria, range statements and evidence indicators. Each performance criterion needs to be demonstrated and evidence must be presented to demonstrate an understanding of all the range dimensions as they relate to the appropriate performance criteria. The difference lies in the fact that the performance criteria are not dependent on work-based evidence for their demonstration.

4. Unlike NVQs, there is a grading system. For an NVQ a candidate is either 'competent' or 'not yet competent' or there is insufficient evidence to confer an award. The possible outcomes for a GNVQ, assuming success, are Pass, Merit and Distinction. Individual GNVQ units, however, are not graded. The award of Merit or Distinction is based on the overall quality of the work presented. For the advanced GNVQ the grades are designed to align with A levels: thus a Distinction equals A/B A level grades A/B; Merit equals grade C; Pass equals grades D/E.

5. Like an NVQ, candidates are required to put together a portfolio of evidence based on the projects, assignments and other activities they have carried out. This is subject to assessment and verification in the same way as for NVQs.

6. In addition to the portfolio of evidence, there is also need for direct observation by centre assessors of the kinds of activities which are not readily documentable by candidates/students. These include oral communications, group participation and some information-technology applications.

7. A key difference to NVQs is the absence of a requirement for performance evidence based on naturally occurring activities in the workplace. The type and range of assessment activities are in many ways similar to those required for existing post-experience courses leading to qualifications such as a Certificate or Diploma in Management Studies.

8. Another key difference to NVQs is the greater emphasis on learning inputs and the provision of a taught programme. Thus, whereas individuals undertaking NVQs are termed 'candidates', GNVQ literature still retains the term 'student'. Although the type of course

offered is open to an individual centre, there is a requirement to provide classroom study and textbooks or open learning materials, in order to cover the breadth of knowledge shown by the range statements within each GNVQ unit.

9. For the mandatory vocational units *only* there are a series of external tests. These are incorporated to quality-assure consistency and reliability in relation to certain aspects of knowledge. They should reinforce knowledge already demonstrated in the candidate's portfolios.

10. Like NVQs, GNVQs are made up of a number of units, and credit can be obtained independently for each unit. There is no requirement to take the units in a pre-determined sequence.

Breadth of GNVQs

The January 1995 *NVQ Criteria and Guidance* (6) states that, while NVQs are based on competence in meeting the standards required for employment in a particular occupation, GNVQs are more broadly based – 'they establish national standards for vocational education, allowing progression into academic or vocational routes for individuals who require an alternative to an occupationally specific award'.

The idea is that the qualifications provide a much broader occupational coverage than is the case with NVQs so that young people do not limit their career options too soon.

The permitted GNVQ areas are much more restricted than are those for NVQs. There are 11 broad NVQ occupational areas, but each of these has been subdivided, leading to an array of lead bodies, associated standards and resulting qualifications.

Thus, within the NVQ occupational category of Providing Business Services, specific occupational areas such as Training and Development and Personnel Management have been identified as well as Management. For GNVQs the range is much more restrictive. Although there are fourteen occupational categories, as opposed to eleven for NVQs these do not provide the basis for subsequent subdivisions. Management is an occupational category – however, as currently conceived it is not possible to subdivide Management into Personnel Management, Training and Development, etc., for the purposes of producing discrete qualifications in these areas.

Also, professional qualifications in specific areas cannot currently be converted into GNVQs unless they demonstrate a broad range of knowledge, understanding and skills across a range of occupational areas. A number do: for example, the Institute of Personnel and Development structure leading to graduateship specifies that 'management' is a core area to be covered. It is a secondary question as to whether anyone would want to convert their professional qualification into a GNVQ.

Higher level GNVQs

There has been some discussion around removing this restriction at the higher levels. The September 1995 NCVQ Consultation Paper on *GNVQs at Higher Levels* (3) suggests that, although higher level GNVQs could follow a similar broad-based model to that of existing GNVQs, there is a need for specialist qualifications in the preparation for, or as a step towards, becoming a professional. Thus one of the questions for consultation asks whether higher level GNVQs should be designed (a) as broad-based foundation qualifications in a vocational area, or (b) as specialist qualifications to meet the progression needs of different students, or (c) the criteria should encompass both types of situation.

Whatever the answer this issue remains largely academic and will probably continue to be so until (a) higher level GNVQs and the broader categories have been introduced, and (b) higher level NVQs are more developed.

Nevertheless, things could happen very quickly. Much depends on the outcome of the consultation process initiated in September 1995. The consultation paper asks for responses to some very basic questions such as:

- Should higher level GNVQs adopt a similar format for specifying outcomes as other GNVQs?
- Should higher level GNVQs consist of units which can be awarded separately to allow credit accumulation and transfer?
- Should core skills be promoted as a significant feature of higher level GNVQs, through mandatory, optional or additional units?
- Should higher level GNVQs be assessed by a combination of portfolios and tests/examinations, depending on the outcomes being assessed?

My guess is that, when launched, higher level GNVQs will not be very dissimilar in format from those already in existence for the lower levels.

Management GNVQs

Until recently there were no GNVQs in Management, the emphasis being on GNVQs in Business Studies. However, following consultation with the NCVQ, employers, professional bodies, industry lead bodies and the education sector, the three awarding bodies of the BTEC, the

City & Guilds and the RSA Examinations Board launched a pilot Advanced GNVQ in Management Studies in September 1994 designed to bring management qualifications into the GNVQ framework. Although the term 'advanced' indicates level 3, it has been suggested that the qualification is in some way 'suspended' between level 3 and a notional level 4. There is also some lack of clarity as to how it relates to existing Management Charter Initiative (MCI) NVQ qualifications

The majority of the participants in the BTEC pilot programme were aged 20–50 years and included women returners, unemployed and part-time employees. This of course is a different group to the 16–19 years age group for whom advanced GNVQs were originally intended.

The content of the GNVQ units in management is more accessible than that of the MCI NVQs, to those individuals accustomed to the format of traditional qualifications. The performance criteria have marked similarities with the learning outcomes of many programmes in this area. The range indicators are reminiscent of indicative content. (See, for example, Unit 2: Organizations and Managers' Roles (Advanced), in *Mandatory Units for Advanced Management Studies* (7: p. 13).)

Relationship of higher level GNVQs in management to other awards

Randall (8), although not referring to this pilot, argues that higher level GNVQs should be developed in appropriate subjects, that higher level GNVQs be more focused than at lower levels (e.g. 'management' rather than 'business studies'), and that Management and Business Studies should be the priority for development work. The same article contends that a clear route of progression from a new GNVQ level 4 in management to higher level NVQs in management should be established.

The author was writing from a Law Society perspective and assuming that GNVQ candidates would not be in employment and could well be undertaking a full-time degree. A GNVQ Management qualification, in combination with one in law, it was argued, could give graduates a marked advantage in today's competitive employment market. As the practice of law becomes more 'business-like', it is suggested that those with a grounding in managerial skills could be particularly attractive to firms of solicitors.

The second assumption made by Randall was that the GNVQ would provide transferable core skills which could be accredited in a way that is recognized by employers and which gives credit towards higher level NVQs. University assessments could be recognized as providing evidence of possession of underpinning knowledge and understanding.

It is commonly assumed that a GNVQ level 4 will align with NVQ level 4. If a level 4 GNVQ is established in management, it will be interesting to see how it cross-maps to:

- Undergraduate degrees with a management component.
- Traditional certificates in management offered by universities and colleges and others.
- MCI 1 standards.

The September 1995 Consultation Paper (3) recognizes that the alignment of standards between level 4 GNVQs and honours degrees needs to be established, and anticipates that they would be designed to share common content in order to facilitate credit transfer between the qualifications. Two interesting options are presented.

- To align the standard of GNVQ level 4 with that of an honours degree, while restricting its coverage (or content) to approximately two-thirds of that of an honours degree.
- To align the standard, content and coverage of GNVQ level 4 with that achieved after the first two years of an honours degree.

The Consultation Paper assumes that a GNVQ level 4 would fulfil the function of, and therefore in time replace, many current diploma courses. We shall see.

It will also be interesting to establish whether existing NVQ D units will suffice for assessment purposes, or whether they will need to be modified.

Stepping stone to NVQs

It is a common assertion that GNVQs should be a stepping stone to NVQs, through the provision of underpinning knowledge and understanding as well as some core skills tested via simulations in a college environment. This perspective is argued for in the September 1995 Consultation Paper (3).

Thus GNVQs could be upgraded, so it is held, once candidates are in work, to an NVQ based on demonstrated competence. It has also been implied that many vocationally oriented diploma courses and qualifications offered by professional bodies have affinities with GNVQs in the sense that underpinning knowledge and understanding (but not competence) are developed and tested therein. The Employment Department chart (Figure 3.1) adopts this perspective in the linking of vocational qualifications with GNVQs in its headings.

This line of thinking, suggesting that an NVQ is a step on from a traditional vocational qualification or GNVQ because it supplements underpinning knowledge and understanding with a demonstration of workplace competence, is hotly contested by many of the professional bodies. However, it would certainly make sense to equate the underpinning knowledge and understanding in GNVQs with that in NVQs.

This would only be realistically possible if each NVQ was mirrored by a GNVQ, i.e. if there were GNVQs in each narrowly defined occupational area.

Capability

Some of the thinking around GNVQs is akin to the emerging notion of capability as formulated by Eraut and Cole (9). They argue that the scope of 'capability' covers the following categories:

* Underpinning knowledge and understanding of concepts, theories facts and procedures.
* The personal skills and qualities required for a professional approach to the conduct of one's work.
* The cognitive process which constitutes professional thinking.
* Understanding of ethical issues pertinent to professional codes of conduct.

> The relationship between *capability* and *competence* has been subjected to a variety of interpretations.
> One way of understanding 'capability' is to perceive it as 'pre-competent' but possessing the potential to become competent.
> Another way is to perceive 'capability' as equivalent to competence.
> A third way is to perceive 'capability' as something more than competence.

Eraut (10) recognizes the potential ambiguity associated with 'capability' and its various connotations. He picks out two definitions from the *Standard Oxford English Dictionary*:

* 'The quality of being capable, of being able to do things'. Eraut feels this is 'almost synonymous with competence'.
* 'An undeveloped faculty or property, a condition capable of being turned into use'. Eraut refers to the fact that the famous landscape architect Capability Brown got his nickname from his habit of saying that the grounds that he was about to 'improve' had capabilities.

Eraut considers that the usefulness of the capability construct for professional education lies in holding these two meanings together in some kind of balance.

Without getting too locked into nuances of meaning, perhaps the key issue is establishing what 'capabilities' can be demonstrated outside of and even before one is in, the workplace – recognizing that the most effective form of vocational learning is experiential and being able to transfer learning to practical situations.

Eraut holds that aspiring professionals can be provided with theoretical knowledge and a critical understanding of concepts, theories and principles, as well as the opportunity to practise skills development, before being let loose inside the workplace.

The Royal Society for the Encouragement of Arts, Manufacturers and Commerce (RSA) has, since 1988, led a national initiative entitled 'Higher Education for Capability' (HEC). The HEC initiative argues that 'capability' is 'an integration of knowledge, skills and personal qualities used effectively and appropriately in response to varied, familiar and unfamiliar circumstances'. In the first edition of its supporting journal (*Capability*) launched in 1994, the Editorial addressed the relationship between 'capability' and 'competence'. It challenged the 'pre-competence' notion of capability by suggesting that 'narrowly defined competences' interpreted as focusing only on 'the capacity to perform' are only part of capability (11).

The Editorial went on to argue that it would be helpful if:

... those driving the national imperative for more vocationally relevant outcomes from education ... signal their acknowledgement that competences include:

(a) the capacity to learn about the changing contexts in which skills are used and to learn from unpredictable consequences of actions taken

and cannot be isolated from

(b) knowledge of the context in which they are being demonstrated
(c) the value systems within which judgements are made about the direction of change and the choice of skills needed to bring change about
(d) the courage, confidence and willingness to learn from failure.

The NCVQ has tried to amplify the notion of 'competence' to take on board the criticisms of the RSA and others.

Capability or potentiality awards

The above set of conditioning factors in relation to capability implies work-related experiences if it is to be demonstrated appropriately. It is taking us away from the sort of qualification which would be of benefit to the mature student or candidate who is unemployed or who does not have a work role which would allow them to generate performance evidence against the national NVQ standards in their chosen occupational area.

Some centres are experimenting with 'capability' or 'pr
competence' awards in specific occupational areas for candidates wh
for various reasons, cannot generate workplace evidence. It is a simil
target group to those individuals accessing the 1994–95 BTEC pil
Advanced GNVQ in Management Studies. As currently constitut
these are not the same as GNVQs, since the GNVQ rubric only perm
awards covering a broad range of occupational areas. However, shou
the guidelines change, there is the distinct possibility of conversion.

I have a personal preference for the term 'potentiality' to designa
pre-competence awards in order to avoid the ambiguity which
associated with 'capability'. A 'potentiality' award would imply to
employer that a candidate who possessed it had sufficient knowledg
understanding and core skills that, with experience, they would
competent in the workplace in their chosen area.

The GNVQ notion is consistent with capability being demonstrat
through a 'potentiality' award. The GNVQ interpretation would
to liken 'capability' to being 'pre-competent', since work-relat
performance has not been assessed. Neverthless, candidates will ha
demonstrated knowledge and understanding across the range, as w
as cognitive skills and an awareness of ethical standards.

GNVQs and professional qualifications

An assumption often made is that higher level GNVQs, when design
to meet professional requirements, would only constitute a st
towards professional accreditation. Final professional qualificati
would be defined by the standards of NVQs or of the professior
bodies.

The September 1995 Consultative Paper (3) suggests that higher lev
GNVQs could be useful in providing the pre-vocational stages of pr
fessional qualifications that are underpinned by large bodies of kno
ledge as well as highly developed cognitive skills. In some instanc
the later stages of the professional qualification could be NVQs. It
also suggested that GNVQ standards could be incorporated into sor
professional qualifications which are not NVQs. By 'pre-vocation
they are referring to the development of an individual's skills ar
abilities before moving into a work role.

The Paper makes specific reference to the engineering professic
whose early stages of qualification are characterized by programm
aimed at developing knowledge, skills and understanding as a founc
tion for subsequent practice. According to the Paper these foundati
stages could be organized into a higher level GNVQ.

It will be interesting to see how the individual professions respond
such suggestions. Many are currently arguing that they see no need t
their existing programmes to be reformatted into 'GNVQ speak' ar

ask what is the added value. If, however, a given profession has decided to go down the competence route and adopt higher level NVQ standards, then there is a much stronger likelihood of converting foundation, pre-vocational programmes into the national framework.

It will also be interesting to see how the universities and higher education institutions respond. A 1995 survey done by the National Association of Teachers in Further and Higher Education (NATFHE) into the further education sector found that 60 per cent of recipients felt that the workload involved in providing GNVQs was extremely heavy – up to a 50 per cent increase above existing duties. The survey found evidence of a dramatic increase in paperwork. This reinforces an independent research survey conducted by the National Foundation for Education Research (NFER) in 1994 for NATFHE into causes of lecturers' stress levels in the further education sector. The introduction of both NVQs and GNVQs were seen to be one of the main areas contributing to stress (12).

In a fast-moving arena, providers will be well advised to keep abreast of developments.

Question 1

You are a provider of NVQ programmes in the management area and are considering offering a GNVQ in Management. Is this a realistic proposition?

For a suggested answer see Chapter 17.

References

1 Debling G. (1995) *Panacea and Parity: Addressing the Myths about NVQs and SVQs* (*Competence and Assessment No. 29*), Employment Department, June.
2 Department for Education (1991) *Education and Training for the 21st Century* London: HMSO.
3 *GNVQs at Higher Levels, a Consultation Paper*, NCVQ, September 1995.
4 *GNVQ Briefing Note*, NCVQ, June 1995.
5 *A Strategy for Vocational Higher Education* (*Competence and Assessment No. 29*), Appendix C of CVCP paper, Employment Department, June 1995.
6 *NVQ Criteria and Guidance*, NCVQ, January 1995.
7 *Mandatory Units for Advanced GNVQ Management Studies*, pilot programme guidelines, NCVQ, September 1994.
8 Randall J. (1995) *National Vocational Qualifications in Higher Education – a Possible Model* (*Competence and Assessment No. 29*), Employment Department, June 1995.
9 Eraut M. and Cole G. (1993) *Assessment of Competence in Higher Level Occupations* (*Competence and Assessment No. 21*), Employment Department.
10 Eraut M. (1994) *Developing Professional Knowledge and Competence*, Falmer Press.
11 HEC (1994) *Capability*, **1**.
12 Reported in NATFHE Journal, October 1995.

4 Input vs output considerations

Objectives

By the end of this chapter you should be able to:

1 Analyse qualification structures by means of the input–output–outcome equation.
2 Distinguish between outcome-driven and input-driven qualifications.
3 Describe how inputs, outputs and outcomes are addressed in NVQs and show how this differs from other qualifications.

The input–output–outcome equation

Qualification structures can be conceived in the form of an equation in which a set of inputs leads to the achievement of a set of outputs and outcomes:

$$x \text{ inputs} = y \text{ outputs} + z \text{ outcomes}$$

These terms may have different connotations depending on one's vantage point. As a consequence, the equation as seen from the perspective of those undertaking a qualification may seem different from the way it is seen by the designers and providers.

From the standpoint of those undertaking a qualification, inputs are the time and effort which they put in on reading, attending workshops and classes, preparing materials for assessment and so on. Outputs are the various forms of 'evidence' which they provide in order to meet the assessment requirements of the qualification. Outcomes are the achievement (or otherwise) of the qualification and other benefits such as access to professional membership, job promotion, personal satisfaction, and so on.

From the perspective of the designers of qualifications, the inputs will consist of the various support mechanisms which need to be in place to enable individuals to reach a position where they can produce the required outputs and achieve the desired outcomes. Outputs take the form of specifying the type of work which should be produced for assessment, be it in the form of assignments, examinations, simulations or evidence from the workplace. Traditional qualifications often talk of 'set pieces' of work, assignments and examinations. NVQ qualifications talk of forms of evidence such as 'naturally occurring' performance evidence from the workplace or simulations. Outcomes are the specification of what needs to be achieved, and to what standard, in order to achieve the qualification. In a number of academic programmes they are expressed in the form of 'behavioural objectives'. In NVQs, they are referred to as 'standards'.

From the perspective of the providers of qualifications, inputs are the resources which they need to make available to satisfy the design requirements. Outputs are the provision of services. Outcomes are the successful (or otherwise) utilization of the services provided.

Outcome-driven vs input-driven qualifications

NVQs have become known as 'outcome-driven' as opposed to 'input-driven' qualifications. The term 'outcome' has been used interchangeably within NVQ circles to cover both outputs and outcomes as defined above. The term 'outcome driven' reflects the fact that the NVQ model is essentially assessment centred. The concern is to measure competence in candidates, competence being defined as performance to the standards expected in employment.

Thus the focus of the qualification system is on candidates demonstrating predetermined outcomes (standards). An element of competence, with its performance criteria and range statements, constitutes a 'standard'. Standards are descriptions of outcomes. They are the results of activity rather than of the inputs and processes which support the outcome. Some outcomes are tangible; they are the physical result of an activity (i.e. a product). But outcomes can be intangible, the result of a cognitive or interactive process, such as making a decision or giving advice.

This is contrasted with the requirement of many academic qualifications which are designated 'input driven' because they include conditions such as attendance at a programme of study for a given number of days at a given time at a given place.

Gilbert Jessup, former Chief Executive of the NCVQ, expressed the input/ output focus in the following terms:

The major impact of the new kind of standards which are being introduced is that they make explicit the outcomes sought in education and training programmes. This contrasts with most previous forms of education and training provision, which has been defined in respect of learning 'inputs' in the form of syllabuses, courses, training specifications and so on. The requirements of qualifications have also been based primarily on the content of the syllabuses and not the other way around. This shift from an 'input-led' system to an 'output-led' system has fundamental implications, both in defining the content of education and training and opening access to different modes of learning. The specification of ou comes provides the key to unlocking the education and training syster (1: p. 11)

The difference in approach is symbolically captured in the termi ology used for those aiming for a qualification. In NVQ terms they a referred to as 'candidates'. This is a deliberate attempt to move aw from the term 'student' which implies someone undertaking a cour of study.

But this oversimplifies the picture. Any qualification structure entai a balance of inputs, outputs and outcomes. It is a gross misrepresent tion to suggest that NVQs consist of no inputs. To do so has resulte in some unforeseen and unfortunate knock-on effects. I recall a we known provider of NVQ programmes informing me a few years a that, with the advent of NVQs, 'learning' was now passé; all that ma tered was demonstration of competence. Such thinking has led son critics to argue that there is no learning in NVQs. In fact, what w meant by my informant was that the NVQ system is not concerne with specifying the 'learning processes' whereby skills and con petences are acquired.

It is also a total distortion to suggest, as does Jessup, that con ventional academic programmes are either not concerned with outpu and outcomes or that they are somehow an 'afterthought' not take into account in the design process.

Academic programme inputs and validation

The conventional academic approach to qualifications has alwa emphasized the importance of the input side of the process. Befo programmes can be offered, they go through a validation proces The validation process is as equally concerned with assessme issues (such as what is being assessed and when) as with inp issues.

Most conventional academic and professional programmes i corporate a programme of study. These include course inputs whic need to be validated by the providing institution or the profession body, or both, as part of the quality-assurance framework. The vali ation process is concerned with ensuring the quality of the followir types of input:

- Course content.
- Number of hours required to deliver the course.
- Number and qualifications of members of the teaching team.
- Appropriateness of the learning environment.

- Back-up resources such as library and media services.
- Reading lists.
- Course materials.
- Sequence of course-unit delivery.

As we shall see, the validation process is not just concerned with the input side of the equation.

NVQ inputs

The literature on NVQs concentrates on output- and outcome-based issues such as:

- Sufficiency of evidence.
- Validity of evidence.
- Types of evidence.
- Reliability of assessment.

It is easy to infer from this that the NVQ system is not concerned with inputs.

Nevertheless, to become an approved NVQ centre, inputs need to be demonstrated. But the emphasis is different from the academic scenario described above. Inputs are:

- Numbers and qualifications of the assessors and verifiers.
- Support mechanisms offered to candidates to enable them to get evidence together.

In a paper published in 1993 (2) I argued that, in complete contrast to the traditional academic approach, the NVQ perspective, in insisting that people should be able to achieve a qualification irrespective of the mode of delivery, was 'neutral' towards the process of learning. It is still true to say that the NVQ structure focuses on ways of objectively and consistently measuring candidates' performances against pre-determined standards rather that the means by which they are achieved. It continues to be more concerned with presentation of evidence in a form acceptable to an assessor rather than in the learning process per se. However, the alleged 'neutrality' of the process of learning needs to be qualified.

There is a defined learning process, but not through providing courses; indeed, there is no NVQ requirement for any taught inputs to be given at all. The process consists, rather, of helping candidates through the learning process of understanding the standards and getting to grips with the sort and quantity of evidence they need to present for assessment. It also addresses the need to help candidates identify what abilities they can currently demonstrate against the standards, and what gaps exist in their competence development.

Guidelines, where they have addressed the question of inputs, have been concerned only with this process of advising candidates how to put an assessment plan together, what the standards mean and what support they can expect. This approach is typified by the development of standards for NVQ Assessors and Verifiers such as:

- D36 – advise and support candidates to identify prior achievements.

Centres need to have accredited advisors who carry out such support.

Many centres providing NVQs offer workshops, but the focus is often around explaining to candidates collectively:

- What standards are.
- What is acceptable evidence.
- What they need to do to put together a portfolio of evidence.

Workbooks and candidate packs are provided, but invariably the focus is on an explanation of process, or an interpretion of the standards for candidates.

Conventional qualifications and outcome considerations

Otter (3) describes a research study premised on the belief that 'the measurement of learning might best be achieved through the description of outcomes (what a learner can do as a result of learning) rather than the more traditional description of learning input (syllabus or course content)'. All the courses I have been involved with in recent years have specified learning outcomes. Indeed, for a number of universities it is now a requirement of validation/approval that they *are* specified. The same condition applies to programmes offered by many professional bodies. For example, each unit within the Institute of Personnel and Development Professional Education Scheme specifies learning outcomes in the following behavioural terms:

- To be able to.
- To understand and explain.

Non-accredited training programmes have also conventionally used similar terminology. Many have long incorporated specific behavioural objectives. One difference to NVQ standards lies in the degree of precision in these specifications.

Atkins, Beattie and Dockrell (4) contend that some of these behaviourally based constructs, which include using words such as 'knowing', 'understanding' and 'appreciating', are 'slippery'. They feel it is difficult to define learning outcomes using such terms and still achieve the required precision. They also argue that it is difficult to achieve an appropriate degree of precision. Too general a level makes a learning outcome impossible to assess; too detailed a level leads to trivialization. Nevertheless, achieving precision in NVQ standards has proved equally problematic. Whatever one's views on the above, it is clear that traditional programmes are not just 'input' driven.

According to Otter (3) the approach to the planning of outcome-driven assessment is patchy in higher education. She found that programmes lacked clarity on the 'outputs' expected of students to meet the stated objectives and that:

> . . . the relationship between the course objectives and what was currently assessed was not always clear . . . There was little evidence of an assessment strategy in many courses. (3)

It should be a function of validation events to identify such short-comings. Those courses with which I have been involved would not be approved without an assessment strategy.

Content issues

The published NVQ standards which make up a qualification specify the 'content' of what has to be assessed. From the perspective of the candidate who receives them they are very content heavy, especially since each performance criterion of each element of each unit must be understood and evidence produced to demonstrate competence. This interpretation of 'content' is, however, different from that used to refer to the 'content' of an academic programme, which is usually held to refer to the body of knowledge that is to be taught/covered and the skills to be practised in lessons, workshops, distance learning packs or whatever.

For academic qualifications a sample only of this content will be assessed. There may also be additional content items covered that are not in the programme documentation. Course documents thus often list 'indicative content' and provide fairly broad statements of learning outcomes which are much more open-ended than the prescriptive nature of standards. This gives scope for considerable flexibility in what is taught and covered.

The syllabus which defines this content often indicates the sequence in which subjects are taught and knowledge addressed. There is no requirement to undertake the NVQ standards in any predetermined sequence, although they are prepackaged into a set of units for accreditation purposes. It is not meaningful to talk of an NVQ syllabus.

The 'knowledge and understanding' specifications in the standard are the closest NVQ equivalent to the course content of a syllabus-led academic programme. However, these are a relatively new requirement. In the past, assessors have had to try to infer 'content' from the performance criteria, range statements and evidence requirements, and define this for the benefit of bemused candidates. The MCI standards are a case in point.

Take MCI II, Element 2.2: Establish and Agree Customer Requirements, from Unit II 2: Monitor, Maintain and Improve Service and Product Delivery. One of the performance criteria is that:

'Agreements satisfy legal and organisational requirements'.

However, what the legal requirements might be is not made specific. Scouring the 'performance evidence required' and 'forms of evidence' sections of the standards takes us no further forward. The 'performance evidence required' section refers to

'The application of relevant legislation . . . in relation to agreements . . . raised to meet customer requirements.'

The 'forms of evidence' section states that 'in the absence of sufficient evidence from performance, questioning can be used to elicit additional evidence of knowledge and understanding of the principles and methods relating to . . . applying relevant items of legislation'.

The 'range indicators' state that specifications must conform to current relevant legislation on:

* Health and Safety at Work etc. Act.
* Sales of Goods Act.
* Care of Substances Hazardous to Health Act.
* Factories Act.
* Office, Shops and Railway Premises Act 1963.
* Other relevant acts related to particular occupational activities.

Are 'specifications' the same as 'agreements'? If they are, then we have discovered the basis for determining the content requirements for that performance criterion. However, there is no guarantee that for other performance criteria the range statements will be so informative.

It is because the standards themselves are expressed in the form of outcomes that it has proved so difficult to dig out the 'content'.

NVQs are unique as a national qualification in terms of the degree of detail that has to be demonstrated and spelt out. It is a requirement that everything is explicit and thus that it is 'transparent' to candidates what they need to do to achieve them.

Nevertheless, this has created some problems for those writing the standards, and some ingenuity is being exercised, especially with regard to 'knowledge and understanding' specifications. Thus the recently rewritten (1994) Training and Development Lead Body specifications (5) refer in a number of elements to 'knowledge of current developments/debates in the field'.

Learned outcomes vs learning outcomes

A useful distinction can be made between 'learning outcomes' and 'learned outcomes'. *Learning outcomes*, in academic terms, are what one should learn as a result of a programme of study. It is not a requirement that each of these are necessarily assessed in practice.

Outcomes of NVQs are *learned outcomes*, i.e. a demonstration that what one has learned from whatever source can be translated into practice at the workplace. There is a much greater emphasis on prior learning than for academic qualifications. On the whole, colleges and universities are concerned with providing learning opportunities, (the effectiveness of which is then assessed), rather than with providing assessment opportunities which might require some learning to achieve.

Nevertheless, many candidates for NVQs will require 'learning events' which go beyond explaining standards and processes. It is not the intention that NVQs at higher levels will be awarded to 'naive pragmatists' who can perform without being able to account for and contextualize their performance.

Providers may offer specific courses in, for example, information technology or selection interviewing skills. There may be tranches of knowledge and understanding, concepts and principles, associated with a given occupational area, which candidates may need to know about in order to achieve the standards required. It is matter of indifference to the NVQ system what these courses are and how well they are delivered, so long as the assessment criteria are met. Individual awarding bodies, however, might be concerned about the quality of programmes offered by their centres and evaluate these as part of their quality-control process. They may carry out a traditional moderation role as well as a verification role; this issue is addressed in greater detail later in this book.

It is indicative that 'learning' as a term is not in the Index of the 1995 *NVQ Criteria and Guidance* (6). Virtually the only references to learning are the following statements, taken from the Introduction:

As NVQs focus on the outcome of successful learning, a range of different learning routes and opportunities are open to individuals.

To be accredited as an NVQ, an award must be, inter alia, 'based on assessment on the outcomes of learning, normally arrived at independently of any particular mode, duration or location of learning'.
'Normally' is another word that has crept in since the publication of the March 1991 *Guide to National Vocational Qualifications* (7). Perhaps NVQs will not turn out to be so neutral to the process of learning as has been the case thus far. Certainly, some centres are offering NVQs which are tied to predetermined learning programmes, especially 'hybrid' awards linked to professional body qualifications.

Anticipated impact of knowledge and understanding specifications

Where, or even whether, knowledge and understanding outcomes should be placed within the standards framework has led to much heated debate. The NVQ position has always been that all outcomes from the system have to do with competence. One view, often expressed, is that if someone has demonstrated competent performance in the workplace, then they must also have, by definition, demonstrated command of the underpinning skills, knowledge and understanding required. No other assessment or evidence will be relevant or necessary. However, this view is not really sustainable at higher levels where it is unlikely that direct evidence of performance will permit one to infer competence over the full range of relevant circumstances.

Whatever the merits or otherwise of the arguments put forward, the NVQ rubric has changed to incorporate separate knowledge and understanding specifications within each statement of competence. The 1995 *NVQ Criteria and Guidance* puts the requirement as follows:

The NVQ statement of competence, which . . . is the authoritative statement of the national standard of performance, has to be accompanied by a knowledge specification. (5: p. 26)

It goes on to say that:

In order to establish that an individual is competent to perform in the situations indicated by the range statements, knowledge and understanding of the activity needs to be assessed. (5: p. 26)

The 1994 *Competence and Assessment Briefing Series No. 10*, entitled *Place of Knowledge and Understanding in the Development of NVQs/SVQs* (8) stated that descriptions of knowledge and understanding which are produced should:

Comparison of academic and NVQ approaches to inputs, outputs and outcomes

Academic	*NVQs*
Inputs	
Programmes are validated	Centres are verified
Focus on taught courses	Focus on advisory services and standards workshops
Provision of syllabuses	Provision of standards
Provision of indicative course content	Provision of knowledge and understanding specifications
Student centred	Candidate centred
Emphasis on subject specialists	Emphasis on qualified assessors and advisors
Importance of learning environment	Not an issue
Importance of back-up resources such as media services and library	Not an issue
Outputs	
Set pieces of work	Performance evidence
Assignments	Naturally occurring
Reports	From the workplace
Simulations	Supplementary evidence
Case studies	Portfolios
Examinations	Observed activities
Outcomes	
Achievement of standards contained in assessment regulations	Demonstration of workplace competence to standards required in employment
Learning outcomes	Learned outcomes

- Be derived from and firmly related to the occupational standards and the actions and decisions within those standards.
- Be distinct from the standards.
- Be justifiable against the elements of competence, their associated performance criteria and range statements.
- Cover that which is relevant to the occupation as a whole, but may be applied to given jobs, contexts or organizations.

There still seems to be some uncertainty as to whether the demonstration of knowledge and understanding is technically part and parcel of the standards of competence, or merely complements them.

Nevertheless, almost inevitably, as knowledge and understanding specifications are incorporated and sharpened up, there will be a need for learning programmes and even syllabuses to be developed by providers, to ensure that they are adequately addressed.

Question 2

You are proposing to become an NVQ centre as a 'bolt-on extra' to the range of traditional taught courses which you offer. Is it permissible to offer these existing courses to NVQ candidates?

For a suggested answer see Chapter 17.

References

1 Jessup G. (1991) *Outcomes – NVQs and the Emerging Model of Education and Training*, Falmer Press.
2 Walton J. (1993) *Vocational Qualifications at Professional Level* (*Institute of Training and Development Occasional Paper No. 1*), ITDO.
3 Otter S. (1992) *Learning Outcomes in Higher Education*, UDACE.
4 Atkins M.J., Beattie J. and Dockrell W.B. *(1994) Assessment Issues in Higher Education*, Employment Department.
5 Training and Development Lead Body Specifications (1994).
6 *NVQ Criteria and Guidance*, NCVQ, January 1995.
7 *Guide to National Vocational Qualifications*, NCVQ, March 1991.
8 Place of Knowledge and Understanding in the Development of NVQs/ SVQs (*Competence and Assessment Briefing Series No. 10*), Employment Department, 1994.

5 Establishing relationships between higher level qualifications: credit accumulation, credit transfer and other considerations

Objectives

By the end of this chapter you should be able to:

1 Establish the role of a clearly articulated credit accumulation and transfer system in determining relationships between qualifications.
2 Differentiate between credit accumulation and credit transfer.
3 Describe the basis of the university credit system.
4 Describe the process needed to be gone through to get a higher level NVQ offered by a particular centre, credit rated on the university tariff.

Introduction

The development of NVQs at levels 4 and 5 has led to a considerable national effort to establish:

- Relationships between NVQs and traditional professional and academic qualifications.
- Coherent pathways which make clear to students/candidates the routes to professional as well as personal development.

At local level, providers are trying to find answers to questions being asked by their students/candidates such as:

- What credits does my NVQ give towards an academic qualification? How does it compare to an undergraduate degree? To a post-graduate qualification?
- What credits does my NVQ give towards a professional accreditation? Can I use it to claim professional membership?
- What credits does my academic qualification give towards an NVQ?

Similarly, the Government is concerned with establishing coherent qualification pathways. To this end it has funded, through the Employment Department, a number of projects aimed at establishing structural relationships between NVQs, academic qualifications and professional awards. As the February 1995 vision document (1) states:

... the aim is to obtain a consensus on the nature of qualifications appropriate for different sectors and on the relationships between them. In particular, areas of possible credit accumulation and transfer would be identified and mechanisms agreed to allow a ready articulation between them.

Credit accumulation and transfer schemes/systems are often treated as a unitary concept, but they in fact consist of two separate aspects. Credit accumulation entails the building up of credits as staging posts towards a qualification. Credit transfer permits credits achieved for one award to be transferred to another award and thereby allows a candidate to be exempt from either a programme of study, or an assessment requirement, or both. Credit transfer thus provides the potential for an individual to bypass a particular component of one award by virtue of having satisfactorily completed components of another award.

The following section provides a background to some of the issues entailed in contributing as a provider to a coherent qualification route that permits mobility for candidates between NVQ and more conventional academic programmes.

Why should a structural relationship be demonstrated between academic post-graduate awards and higher level NVQ awards?

Atkins et al. (2) identify 'specific vocational preparation usually linked to entry to a profession' as a key purpose for higher education. It is this arena which is most akin to NVQ provision. In achieving this purpose they also distinguish between undergraduate provision and post-graduate provision, and between initial post-graduate training and continuing professional development courses. They also refer to 'academic' post-graduate programmes, which for them are an extension of the field of study undertaken for a first degree and are not related to this particular purpose.

Centres which wish to:

- contribute towards a coherent qualification route which bridges the academic/NVQ divide
- provide logical development opportunities for individuals

need to demonstrate to their candidates some form of structural relationship that enables comparisons to be made between:

- NVQ awards.
- Academically based vocational (professional) qualifications related to specific vocational preparation and progression.

If relationships are not made clear, not only is it impossible to develop a coherent qualification pathway, but also there is no way of judging comparability of achievement between people who have gone through one system and those who have gone through another. It becomes difficult for prior achievement in one scheme to be recognized in the other. This in turn can lead to two independent systems of qualifications running in parallel without any cross-reference, and with the exponents of each perceiving the other to be less valuable. Thus, for example, a respondent on a recent project I was involved in argued that, in her opinion, 'the academic system carries much excess baggage exemplified by the mysticism and self-generating vocabulary of the intelligentsia. The S/NVQ system gets rid of this baggage to reveal what the candidate can actually do'. Similar pejorative comments have been made by academics about NVQ qualifications.

The distinction between post-experience and post-graduate

One of the first issues that needs to be clarified in establishing relationships is the difference between a post-experience and a post-graduate programme/qualification. The distinction is somewhat technical but it is current in university circles. It is vital to understand why it has been necessary to develop it and what the implications for candidates and providers are.

Post-experience programmes and qualifications

'Post-experience' is a generic term used to cover qualifications which require of entrants some prior work-based/occupational experience. It can apply to any vocational qualification, including NVQs, irrespective of level. Entry onto a post-experience programme can be achieved without necessarily having obtained any accredited qualifications.

There are a variety of bodies who have been involved in the awarding of post-experience qualifications in the professional/management field. These include professional bodies such as the Institute of Management, the Institute of Personnel and Development, the Institute of Administrative Management, as well as more broadly based bodies such as the BTEC, the City & Guilds and the Royal Society for the Encouragement of Arts, Manufactures and Commerce (RSA). Conventionally their programmes have been delivered through approved centres, these being primarily, but not exclusively, colleges and universities in the further and higher education sectors.

Some post-experience qualifications will also be post-graduate awards as described below. Some also will be of post-graduate level, although this would have to be demonstrated to the satisfaction of the accrediting agencies.

Post-graduate programmes and qualifications

'Post-graduate' is a term used to cover a number of aspects. What constitutes a *post-graduate level* is that candidates demonstrate intellectual abilities that are not performance-in-role specific. Typical university requirements include the ability to:

- Argue rationally and draw independent conclusions based on a rigorous, analytical and critical approach to data, demonstration and argument.
- Reflect on the interrelationship between theory and practice.
- Demonstrate some originality in reflection.
- Demonstrate a capacity for initiating change in response to earlier reflections.

These are cognitive abilities and are distinct from any subject-specific knowledge and understanding. They are akin to the general educational objectives of the old Council for National Academic Awards (CNAA) (3).

In late 1994, I organized a workshop at which a number of accredited NVQ assessors, who were also responsible for delivering university programmes, looked at some NVQ level 4 portfolios in order to establish whether they were of post-graduate level. After the assessment activity the assessors brainstormed the criteria they had used to determine what for them would constitute a post-graduate level NVQ portfolio. These were subsequently composited as follows.

1 The ability to reflect critically on the totality of an occupationally relevant group of competences in the light of knowledge of the field and practitioner experience.
2 The ability to relate critical reflections to existing comprehensive conceptual frameworks, and generate new frameworks should existing frameworks not be adequate.
3 The ability to relate critical reflections and conceptual constructs to practical professional situations at an appropriate level, and through analysis to determine sound courses of action.
4 The ability to present, and to argue logically, proposals for courses of action based on models of good practice.
5 The possession of a body of knowledge and conceptual frameworks of sufficient depth and breadth to be confident that reflections, proposals and actions are adequately grounded.

The first four criteria are generic cognitive skills. They are general criteria applicable across professions. The fifth criterion represents knowledge, including that of conceptual frameworks, which would be specific to each occupational area.

There are also rules governing the features of *post-graduate qualifications*. The original notion of a post-graduate qualification was that it would be a continuation of a first degree, enabling students to pursue their studies in their first discipline and achieve greater insight into and subject understanding and 'mastery' of that subject. Such post-graduate programmes often entailed merely the production of a dissertation in the appropriate subject area. Although many such programmes still exist, a large number of students are undertaking post-graduate certificate, diploma and masters programmes' in a subject totally unrelated to their first degree. Additionally, an increasing number of post-experience students without a first degree are accessing these post-graduate programmes as universities modify their entrance requirements.

Post-graduate awards are limited to the academic higher education sector. Post-graduate certificates, diplomas and master's qualifications can normally only be obtained through the national network of universities. However, there is an increasing trend for colleges to operate under licence to a university and accordingly offer university-accredited qualifications to their students. Also, it is possible for non-university qualifications to get a credit rating from national bodies such as the Open University Validation Services.

What is meant by credit accumulation and transfer frameworks and what are their implications?

The concept of credit accumulation and transfer (CAT) is intrinsic to the NVQ model. Qualifications are composed of a number of units, each of which can be accredited separately.

Units must be designed so that they may be offered for separate assessment and certification, enabling them to be recorded as credits within the national credit accumulation and transfer system. (4)

Within the NVQ system it is possible for units developed by one lead body to be incorporated into the qualification structure of another occupational area. Thus level 4 Training and Development qualifications import some Management Charter Initiative (MCI) I Units. Such MCI units achieved by candidates for the Training and Development qualification could be transferred as credits towards the MCI award.

Whereas the concept of CAT is intrinsic to the NVQ model, it is a relatively new concept in the academic world. Many of the 'old' universities have no concept of CAT. The notion has greater currency for the new universities (old polytechnics) where the old CNAA developed a credit structure in 1986. Even where a CAT framework is followed, there is no automatic entitlement that credits achieved by an individual at one centre within the university structure will be recognized by another centre. This is contrary to the NVQ model. However, the development of CAT arrangements in respect of qualifications since the first pilot scheme was launched by the CNAA in 1986, has led to far greater flexibility in terms of entry onto post-graduate programmes.

How can one provide access for non-graduates to a post-graduate pathway leading to a master's degree?

Before CAT was established it was difficult, for example, to gain exemption for any part of a taught master's degree which conventionally consists of three stages: certificate, diploma and master's. The only issue in respect of post-experience qualifications concerned whether non-standard entrants (i.e. those without a degree) could gain access to the first stage of a post-graduate pathway. Some professional post-experience programmes were treated as being of equivalent status to a degree in terms of entry.

The establishment of CAT has provided a mechanism to enable the additional consideration of whether successful completion of a professional post-experience programme can lead to access to the intermediary and later stages of post-graduate pathways.

University CAT frameworks, based on the old CNAA framework, aim to provide additional entry opportunities to higher education and continuing professional education programmes, by enabling students to gain the maximum possible exemption for qualifications and learning already achieved. They also permit mechanisms whereby, instead of studying on a designated course, people are able to negotiate their own programmes and achieve accreditation for prior learning. In order to facilitate this, all courses, and units within courses, are allocated a credit rating which can be recognized as having a transfer value for entry on to another programme of study. There are a set number of credits to be achieved for specific awards.

The university CAT framework provides an important mechanism for bridging the vocational/academic divide. Its ethos is also congruent with that of its NVQ counterpart in terms of opening up access to qualifications.

General background to credit rating and university entry requirements

The conventional way of giving academic credit ratings has been to develop a numerical scale and then to develop a set of criteria – often with a preponderance of input criteria such as hours taught – which constitute the basis for gaining credits on the scale.

A good example is the old CNAA Undergraduate and Master (M) level scale, which in general terms many of the new universities still follow:

The old CNAA CAT scheme adopted the following grading structure:

Level 1 Corresponds to the first year of a full time honours degree.

Level 2 Corresponds to the second year of a full time honours degree.

Level 3 Corresponds to the final year of a full-time honours degree.

Level M Corresponds to post-graduate study at master's level.

It also developed a points system for the attainment of post-graduate qualifications:

35 M points Equates to a post-graduate certificate.
70 M points Equates to a post-graduate diploma.
120 M points Equates to a master's degree.

Many universities subdivide the credits into units. Thus, typically, an M level Unit is classified as ten M credits which equates to forty input hours and eighty additional self-directed learning hours for each student. A half-unit thus becomes five credits with twenty input hours and forty additional self-directed learning hours. Accordingly post-graduate certificates, diplomas and master's degrees are made up of a number of units and half-units which collectively add up to the requisite number of points on the scale. Similar rules apply to the old CNAA undergraduate scale. However, there is no universal consensus amongst universities on the credit value of post-graduate awards or of the credit value of individual units.

NVQs, as they are currently constituted, are predominantly outcome driven, not input driven. It would not be possible to establish a credit rating based on input criteria such as the number of taught hours, since the NVQ rules demand that candidates can achieve an award independent of a process of learning such as class attendance.

Like the academic qualifications referred to above, NVQ awards are made up of a set of units, the satisfactory completion of each of which constitutes a credit towards the final qualification. Discounting the input–outcome debate for the moment, credits on the appropriate academic credit level scale could theoretically be given for the whole NVQ qualification or for the individual units which make up the qualification.

General and specific credits

The situation is further complicated by the distinction between general and specific credits on the academic scale. In essence, general credits indicate that one has been credited with having achieved a level of attainment on a given credit scale without the credits being specifically attached to a qualification – indeed the credits are not necessarily in a related field; whereas specific credits mean that one has been credit rated at the same level and in the same subject area and covering the same ground as a given qualification. The key difference is that specific credits can more easily provide exemptions from earlier stages of a qualification. Seventy specific credits at M level in Human Resource Development could mean that an individual has the entry qualifications to go straight onto the final master's stage of a qualification without taking the post-graduate diploma.

There is, however, no guarantee that possession of specific credits will lead to direct access. Most university programmes include a caveat that applicants should be able to meet the learning demands of a given programme, and admissions tutors always have the right to refuse entry. Similarly, it is possible, depending on the stated entry requirements, for individuals to gain direct access to the later stages of a qualification with general credits, or indeed with no credits at all.

The latter case could apply in exceptional circumstances where the admissions tutor felt that a candidate's prior experiential learning was such as to allow him or her direct access. It could also apply where a candidate has an award such as an NVQ at level 4 which has no official general or specific credit rating, but where it is felt that a candidate had covered sufficient ground to bypass a stage of the qualification route. Some members of the University Forum for Human Resource Development have gone on record to say that candidates for a Post-Graduate Diploma in this subject could bypass the Post-Graduate Certificate stage if they had an NVQ level 4 using Training and Development Lead Body (TDLB) standards and they could demonstrate to the admissions tutor that they could meet the learning demands of the programme.

If it was felt that a formal credit rating of NVQs was desirable, of significance would be the number of credit points awarded. A general credit rating of, say, twenty points might have no meaning if one was seeking direct access onto a masters's programme for which seventy specific credits was an entry requirement. A specific credit rating of twenty points might be more marketable, but only if one could show the relationship between the learning accomplished to achieve those credits and the units on the university programme to which an individual was seeking access. If there were a correlation, twenty specific credits could lead to exemption from two university units of ten M points each.

Establishing a benchmark for a specific, national, post-graduate credit pointing for NVQs is troublesome, since each university designs its own programmes. Thus in the human resource development field, although there is a common body of knowledge, different universities focus on different aspects and, even where there is some commonality of approach, each university designs its own units which packages the body of knowledge differently.

Also, as indicated above, there is no consensus among universities as to the number of credit points which make up a unit, or even an award. For example, a unit at Thames Valley University is worth fifteen M points whereas a similar unit at South Bank University is worth ten M points. A Post-graduate Diploma at London Guildhall University is worth eighty M points, while one at Wolverhampton University it is worth seventy M points.

Accreditation of prior learning

To be enabled to bypass any part of a qualification requires some form of accreditation of prior learning (APL) arrangement. One form of prior learning is prior 'certificated' learning by which, for example, qualifications gained through one awarding body can be recognized as a credit for another programme of learning.

The underlying principle is to give recognition for comparable achievement. To provide the flexibility necessary to allow for a wide variety of individual circumstances, a general credit rating is assigned to each of the various awards. It is then open to the receiving centre to adjust this in the light of the particular circumstances (e.g. relevance, congruence and time elapsed since completion), to arrive at a specific credit rating for the individual student and/or programme of study.

The Open University Validation Service (OUVS), taking over the CNAA's credit awarding role, has also recognized some professional qualifications as being the equivalent of a post-graduate award through CAT. For example, successful completion of the Institute of Personnel and Development's professional programme is seen as the equivalent of a post-graduate diploma in terms of credit rating.

The CAT philosophy also permits accreditation of prior experiential learning (APEL). This is a way of presenting 'uncertificated' learning in a form that can be assessed with reasonable academic objectivity so that it may be formally accredited and accumulated towards an academic award. The APEL procedure typically involves a sequence of four stages, and the learner is responsible for the first three of these:

1 Systematic reflection on experience of significant learning.
2 Identification of significant learning expressed in precise statements which constitute claims to the possession of knowledge and skills.

3 Synthesis of evidence to support the claim made.
4 Assessment of the award for academic credits.

Confusion over credit rating

There is currently much confusion in this area as you can imagine from the complexity of the system described above. Take, for example, the Certificate in Management. It is possible to obtain from an awarding body such as BTEC, an MCI-endorsed Certificate in Management which is a competence-based post-experience qualification. It is possible to obtain from a university an MCI-endorsed Post-graduate Certificate in Management which attracts thirty-five M points. Although there may be overlap and much common purpose between university requirements for their post-graduate certificate awards and MCI certificate level accreditation, the two should not be regarded as synonymous. The difference between an MCI-endorsed Certificate and a university 'competence-based' Certificate relates to additional 'cognitive' and input requirements associated with the attainment of post-graduate M point credits.

Credit rating

Credit rating is a service offered by some individual universities as well as by national agencies such as the OUVS. It involves judging the extent to which the learning achieved within professional qualifications, training courses, short courses and other types of programme meets the requirements of a first or master's degree. A programme will be assigned a general credit value according to the amount of higher education learning that it is judged by the accrediting body to achieve.

According to the *OUVS Credit Rating Handbook* (5) the OUVS credit rating arrangements are based on the principle that:

. . . appropriate learning wherever it occurs but providing it can be assessed, may be recognized for credit towards higher education awards.

The OUVS Handbook emphasizes that the key questions in credit rating are:

• What is learnt?
• How is the learning assessed?
• How is the quality and consistency of the learning and assessment maintained?

Thus the programme put forward by an organization for credit rating need not be 'classroom' orientated or offered on a 'taught' basis. For example it is possible to credit rate programmes that take place through learning in the workplace provided that the learning is at a higher education level and can be assessed, is adequately managed and supervised and is subject to close monitoring by the organization.

Basic steps for NVQ providers seeking a post-graduate credit rating

1 Contact credit rating organizations such as the OUVS and obtain their guidelines.
2 Contact a local university and establish whether they offer a credit-rating service.
3 Find out what the scale of charges is.
4 Make personal contact to clarify details. Establish how much help the accrediting body will give you.
5 Establish whether you will get a general or a specific credit rating. Try to determine the market currency of the credit rating. If you are only getting, say, ten post-graduate points, what does this mean in practice?
6 Be prepared to modify your programme/assessment requirements in order to demonstrate that learning is at a higher education level. What the accrediting body will be looking for as a minimum is evidence that assessments meet the post-graduate level criteria listed earlier (see p. 54).

It may be that obtaining a credit rating is not of great significance if individual candidates are able to access the appropriate stage of a university programme on the basis of their portfolio evidence being accredited through a university APL mechanism. Establish what different universities' attitudes are towards APL. Be prepared to get mixed messages!

References

1 *A Vision for Higher Level Vocational Qualifications*, Employment Department, February 1995.
2 Atkins M.J., Beattie J. and Dockrell W.B. (1993) *Assessment Issues in Higher Education*, Employment Department, March.
3 *CNAA Handbook*, 1993.
4 *Guide to National Vocational Qualifications*, NCVQ, March 1991.
5 *OUVS Credit Rating Handbook*.

6 Hybrid programmes that bridge the academic–vocational divide

Objectives

By the end of this chapter you should be able to:

1 Describe what is meant by a 'hybrid programme'.
2 Differentiate between different types of hybrid programme.
3 Indicate why such programmes are currently being considered at the higher levels of qualifications.
4 Identify some of the issues associated with providing hybrid programmes leading to qualifications based on different design and assessment methodologies.
5 Determine the advantages and disadvantages of being involved in a hybrid programme.

Classification of hybrid programmes

The introduction of NVQs and GNVQs, both of which have different approaches to traditional vocationally oriented academic qualifications, has meant that there are now three vocational qualification systems operating in the UK. This in turn has led to the possibility of programmes operating across these systems, importing values and ideas from each.

As Debling has put it:

> . . . to secure an effective workforce we need the best of traditional education together with NVQs and SVQs . . . We need to be more effective in developing the broader skills and attributes of individuals as well as insuring that they perform more effectively in their specific occupations at work. (1: p. 7)

This does not entail replacing one qualification another or with arguing that one is better than another. They serve different purposes.

A 'hybrid' programme is one that cuts across two or more of these qualification systems, providing the opportunity for candidates or students to achieve more than one award, or dual certification. It should not be confused with joint honours degrees or suchlike where only one qualification is provided at the end of the day.

Hybrid programmes should also not be confused with mechanisms whereby the achievement of one award leads to credits towards or exemptions from another qualification undertaken at a different moment in time and perhaps at another institution. Hybrid qualifications go beyond establishing relationships for student or candidate progression. They entail either:

- Programmes of learning/modes of assessment provided by a given institution, which are jointly recognized by different awarding and examining bodies and lead to joint awards simultaneously conferred. *Or*
- Arrangements devised by a given provider in which the assessment methodology in one qualification is congruent with and contributes to assessment in another linked qualification offered by the same provider.

One interesting issue of terminology arises. Are participants on hybrid programmes 'students' or 'candidates'? Perhaps we need to invent another term, that of 'student-candidates'.

Programmes in which students/candidates are confronted with an identical amount of workload to that they would face if each qualification were to be undertaken independently are not hybrids. There need to be significant simplifying bridging processes without these being at the expense of the integrity of the outcomes.

Within the NVQ structure it is possible to gain more than one award through using standards from more than one lead body. An example would be a programme whereby candidates gain an NVQ level 4 in Training and Development using Training and Development Lead Body (TDLB) standards *and* an NVQ level 4 in Management using Management Charter Initiative (MCI) standards.

Within the traditional academic/professional vocational qualification area, dual certification (Figure 6.1) has been possible for a number of years. For instance, professional bodies have often engaged in joint validation events with universities in order to approve post-graduate university programmes which lead simultaneously to an award conferred by a professional body. One such, reported by Randall (2), is the Law Society's Legal Practice Course, which is offered by a number of

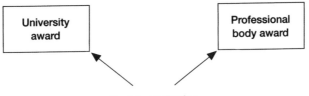

Figure 6.1 One programme of learning can lead to two awards being simultaneously conferred by two different awarding/examining bodies

higher education institutions. The courses are approved by the Law Society, which also appoints external examiners on the nomination of the institutions. However, in all instances, the courses lead to diplomas awarded by the providing institution.

Although both the examples given above afford opportunities for dual accreditation, they are operating within a discrete qualification system with similar values and approaches to inputs, outputs and outcomes. Therefore they do not count as hybrids, given the definition above.

The Institute of Management (IM) Certificate and Diploma in Management (Competent Manager Programmes) are examples of genuine hybrid programmes (Figure 6.2). Both Certificate and Diploma programmes are designed to last approximately one year, but participants are permitted to submit work within an eighteen-month period without the need for separate registration. The courses contain learning inputs based on open learning material and residential workshops for each of the modules. Assessment for the Diploma in Management and the NVQ level 5 includes written assignments, an integrative project and a personal effectiveness interview. It also requires completion of a portfolio of evidence proving competence against the occupational standards for management (MCI II).

Another example, reported by Walton (3), is the South Bank University programme which I helped to design and which provides a route to post-graduate qualifications in human resource development and NVQs in training.

As NVQs and perhaps GNVQs develop at levels 4 and 5, it can be expected that such new style hybrid programmes which attempt to incorporate academic, competence and professional requirements will become increasingly common. This will be in response to an increasing demand from students and candidates seeking recognition across the vocational systems. They will seek accreditation of both their competence in the workplace and their academic ability to handle concepts, draw upon a broad-based body of knowledge and develop insights from a vocationally oriented course of study. They will also be seeking professional membership. This is not to say that competence is not addressed on academic vocational programmes or that concepts are not covered on NVQs. However, there are substantial differences in the ways that these aspects are addressed and the priorities and importance that are given to them in the two approaches.

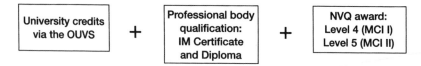

Figure 6.2 An example of a true hybrid programme

This demand is creating, and will continue to create, an enormous challenge for programme designers. This is because of the substantial differences in assessment methodology and ways of thinking about learning processes between the qualification systems. As a former colleague of mine has often stated: 'It's like comparing chalk and cheese'.

Added value for participants of hybrid programmes

The establishment of hybrid arrangements across qualification structures can add considerable value to the learning process. It enhances the learning of individuals if they can translate their learning to the workplace and if their learning from the workplace can be translated into explanatory conceptual frameworks. A true hybrid programme integrating academic and NVQ approaches enables the practitioner to go round the Kolb experiential learning cycle from two different perspectives.

Perspective A in Figure 6.3 show the cycle as commonly presented and understood. The theory holds that we learn most effectively from our experiences. Each experience should cause us to reflect on what took place; the reflection should lead us to generate concepts to explain what happened and what we might do differently in future; from the conceptualization we should experiment with new approaches; such new approaches generate new experiences on which we can reflect; and so the cycle continues, leading to richer and broader experience and expertise. If we start from experience, then the model leads to a 'theory-out-of-practice' approach to learning. If perceived in such a way then it is potentially a reactive model with the implication that we learn from experience only.

The cycle is also neutral with regards to where individuals get their ideas for 'abstract conceptualization' from. Where do people look for the new theoretical frameworks that will enable them to do things differently in the future?

It is possible to turn the Kolb cycle on its head and generate a

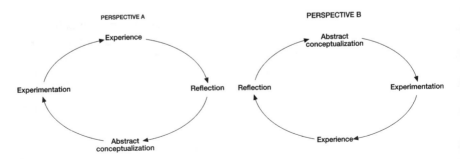

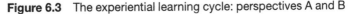

Figure 6.3 The experiential learning cycle: perspectives A and B

'theory-to-practice' approach. Let us assume that an individual goes through a developmental learning experience in which concepts are generated within a subject-specific domain that generates new possibilities for action that previously the learner had not conceived of as appropriate or possible within their role. Such concepts can even transform their world view. The model now looks as shown in perspective B in Figure 6.3. This is the perspective of traditional post-experience vocational qualifications at the higher levels.

General points about establishing relationships between qualifications systems

The Committee of Vice Chancellors and Principals (CVCP) (4) suggests that issues for universities and professional institutions to consider include:

- The likely impact of higher level S/NVQs, especially in the post-academic stages of professional formation and in continuous professional development (CPD).
- The possible implications for professional formation of higher level GNVQs/GSVQs.
- The need to articulate the relationship (and possible overlap) between current professional qualifications and S/NVQs.

At present, higher level GNVQs have not yet taken off but, following the 1995 consultation process, developments could be speedy.

Otter (5) suggests that there are several possible relationships between higher education courses and programmes and S/NVQs, extending right across the higher education spectrum. This range is from initial qualification, both non-vocational and vocational, to continuing professional development, where she believes some of the practical and conceptual difficulties of working with NVQs may more easily be resolved. This, of course, is the arena on which this handbook is focusing.

The possible relationship between systems includes, for her:

- An *indirect, informing* relationship, where occupational standards inform the higher education curriculum, but where assessment is not to NVQ standards and no NVQ accreditation is sought.
- A *direct* relationship, where NVQ units might be used to award credit for periods of work experience, or sandwich placement, or for degrees/diplomas which include, or are based on, work-based learning.
- A *direct* relationship for those professional post-experience and continuing professional development courses which involve students in professional practice. This could lead to dual accreditation.

She also considers that establishing direct relationships is easier for post-experience students at higher levels because of the opportunities they have for generating work-related evidence.

It is impossible to develop an integrated hybrid qualification without some method of establishing a relationship between NVQ levels and outcomes and those developed for academically based vocational (professional) qualifications. Each of these themes are pursued below.

Relationship between levels

Hybrid programmes require judgments to be made about respective levels of qualification. If one is offering a dual award that spans the academic and NVQ qualification systems, does the level of, say, a post-graduate certificate equate to an NVQ level 4 or to an NVQ level 5?

From the perspective of higher education institutions it is easier to establish meaningful relationships with NVQs for post-experience programmes than for undergraduate programmes. This is because the qualifications are often targeted at individuals who are

- In work.
- Possess similar job roles.

Thus in the management area, post-graduate certificates have over the years been aimed at relatively junior managers, whereas post-graduate diplomas have been targeted at more experienced staff. This is paralleled by the MCI role descriptors. Thus the MCI II standards:

. . . define the role requirements for those managers who are responsible for converting an organization's strategy and policy into operational objectives, perhaps to be handed on to other managers, operational teams and in some cases functional and technical specialists.

Those higher education institutions which have developed hybrid programmes in the management area have accordingly, on the basis of job role criteria, linked:

- MCI I (NVQ level 4) with their post-graduate certificate in management. *and*
- MCI II (NVQ level 5) with their post-graduate diploma in management/management studies.

Relationship between outcomes

The universities have not gone on to say that an NVQ at level 4 or a level 5, independently undertaken, is at post-graduate level. This i partly because, to date, the NVQ assessments are not measuring th same things as would be expected of a post-graduate student. It ha also to do with academic perceptions of the quality of outcomes fror NVQ candidates. Views on this may change as the NVQ assessmer rubric changes at the higher levels.

For example, Randall (2) contends that the difficulty with NVQ may be more apparent than real at the higher levels. At higher leve there is much closer relationship between traditional academic qual fications and NVQs than there is at lower levels. This is because th 'body of knowledge-possession' which must be measured become greater, and the understanding which must be assessed, mor complex.

Remember that NVQs are concerned with the ability to conform t predetermined standards of competence in the workplace. The em phasis is on *performance*. Until recently it has not been a requiremer that knowledge and understanding are assessed independently.

On the other hand, many post-experience academic qualification and related professional qualifications have, in the past, primaril focused on what, in NVQ terms, are only the underpinning skills The knowledge and understanding required for effective performanc These have been assessed by a mix of examinations, written assigr ments and course-based skills exercises/simulations. Many pos graduate and master's programmes offered at universities and othe higher education institutions have not been concerned at all wit effective performance.

However, as the CVCP has recognized (4), there is particular scop for integrating the academic and competence-based approaches t education in post-graduate and post-experience professional course: This is a position I have also previously articulated:

It is possible to develop a qualification framework which bridges th academic/NVQ divide . . . academics will need to accept that student can benefit from a structure that emphasizes work-based assessment: which provides individuals with detailed access to the criteria by whic performance is assessed, and which enable individuals to bring forwar their own relevant evidence of competence. They will need to accept tha the competence-based approach is not inconsistent with the develop ment of broad concept formation, and the academic standards are nc threatened. Similarly the advocates of the NVQ system must recogniz that a 'mere competence approach' might well be challenged – fairly c otherwise – by academics as being too narrow in focus for higher leve qualifications. There is increasing evidence that there is a meeting c minds and that innovative approaches to overcome barriers are being developed across the spectrum. (3: pp. 25–6)

The issue for programme designers is to judge the degree of overlap between academic assessment requirements for a post-graduate award and the evidence requirements to demonstrate that the performance criteria of the NVQ standards have been fully met.

What are the core features required for each award? What are the specific requirements which do not overlap?

In practice, what has happened in most hybrid programmes designed by higher education institutions is that:

- Assignments have been designed which, in addition to meeting academic requirements in terms of breadth and depth of content, enable students to generate evidence against a range of standards.
- Full demonstration of the standards has become an extra assessment ingredient. This has been accomplished by getting candidates to produce a full portfolio of performance-related evidence.

(See Figures 6.4 and 6.5.)

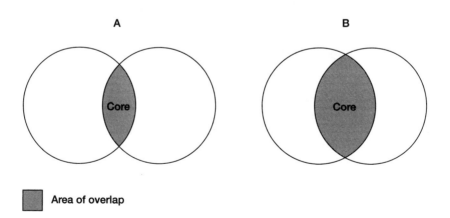

Figure 6.4   Extent of overlap of requirements

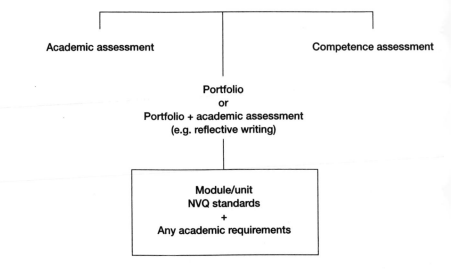

Figure 6.5 Diagrammatic representation of the dual accreditation model

Avoiding double jeopardy

How can one accommodate standards from one qualification syste
maintain the integrity of the other, and yet somehow simplify a
organize assessment arrangements so that it doesn't happen that ca
didates are subject to a double assessment load? That is the challen
for designers of hybrid programmes.

Because NVQs are measuring national standards, which technica
should be the same wherever they are have been assessed, many
these assessment issues originate from the 'traditional' provider sic
For example, each university is responsible for the standards of
awards, and the content will differ from institution to institution. T
questions for a given provider are:

- How can academic assessments be tailored to meet NVQ
  requirements?
- Do NVQ assessment requirements need to be amplified to meet the
  requirements of university and professional programmes, and if so
  how?

NVQ providers outside the university system have not offer
hybrid programmes which simultaneously lead to universi
awards since, unless they are operating under franchise, they are n
empowered to do so.

Practical problems associated with hybrid programmes

There are a number of tensions in a hybrid programme:

1   To achieve two awards simultaneously conferred requires provision of inputs and completion of assessments over and above what would be required if undertaking just one qualification. This can put a *strain on candidates* and deleteriously affect completion rates. Some individuals undertaking hybrid programmes have complained of them being 'too big'. It can also put a *strain on assessors* who, in addition to having to undertake additional assessment activities, are looking at work from different perspectives.

2   The different awarding and examining bodies associated with a hybrid qualification might have *different measures of success*. For example, universities' quality measures include the number and percentage of candidates completing a programme within a stated period, whereas the NVQ awarding body guidelines emphasize the importance of candidates completing at their own pace.

3   *Quality-control measures will differ* between awarding and examining bodies. Traditional programmes have been measured by input criteria such as the number of hours studied, the quality of teaching, the adequacy of learning resources (such as libraries and teaching rooms), as well as output criteria such as the quality of work. NVQs focus primarily on quality of assessment and the qualifications needed by assessors to assess.

4   There may be a need for *two separate assessment exercises* – of competence for NVQ purposes and of cognitive skills and domain-specific knowledge for university purposes. Although, increasingly, there is an expectation that knowledge and understanding and concepts should be demonstrated within a higher level NVQ, they are, given the NVQ ethos, inevitably subordinated to performance. My feeling is that non-performance-specific knowledge and understanding need to be demonstrated and assessed separately in order to meet the requirements of university and other non-NVQ awards. This is because many instances of knowledge and understanding covered on hybrid programmes will be 'domain-specific' (i.e. cover the whole domain of an occupational area) and not be contextualized against particular elements within the NVQ standards.

5   Traditional programmes have been overseen by external examiners or moderators. NVQ programmes are overseen by external verifiers. If these *roles of overseeing are held by different people*, then there is a risk that they may view a given candidate's work differently. There is also a problem for the provider of establishing additional relationships.

6   *Academic units* which make up a post-graduate award are not the same thing as *NVQ units*. Although programmes can be designed to

ensure substantial correspondence between taught inputs for the pos
graduate award and NVQ standards, it is not likely that there will be
perfect match.

Hybrid programmes that are not simultaneously completed and assessed

A number of providers who have experimented with hybrid pr
grammes involving an integrated assessment strategy have move
away from this approach described above. The reasons are related t
the tensions described above and a feeling that the approach is to
demanding for many student-candidates.

A model that is increasingly emerging in the university sector is t
maintain links between the NVQ and traditional vocational qual
fication systems, whilst separating out the assessment as shown i
Figure 6.6. There are a number of points which are worth drawin
out.

- The first stage is, in many ways, similar to that adopted for GNVQs.
- Student-candidates complete their post-graduate assessment befor
  moving on to put together their full portfolio of evidence for the NVQ.
- Student-candidates have the opportunity, should they so wish, to
  achieve a post-graduate award without going on to get their NVQ
  qualification.

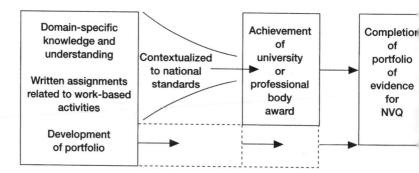

Figure 6.6 Staged approach to accreditation

Getting a hybrid programme approved

NVQ awarding bodies are, on the whole, disinterested in whethe
or not one is offering a hybrid programme. Their primary concern i
that the requirements for the NVQ qualification are satisfied, i.e

whether there are sufficient accredited assessors and verifiers and what the nature is of the support systems for candidates.

For universities the situation is totally different. Every new programme has to go through an individual university's own quality-assurance process. In 'university speak', this means getting it validated. Within the higher education system one of the most daunting and stressful experiences that academic members of staff are subjected to is presenting and defending a programme for the external scrutiny of a validation event. The panel typically consists of internal representatives from the 'home' institution and external subject experts. Often the internal representatives have no subject expertise in the programme area and are there to ensure that programme documentation and the overall structure and underlying philosophy meet institutional and academic requirements. One often cannot anticipate the line of questioning, which can turn out to be highly eccentric and quite capricious.

Each extra ingredient that is added to the equation complicates the situation and makes the outcome that more uncertain. If one is seeking professional recognition and accreditation from the validation event as well as institutional approval, there is a degree of risk that what the professional body are seeking does not coincide with the needs of the institution.

This is relatively manageable compared to the attempt to squeeze through an acceptance of an NVQ in conjunction with an academic award. In respect of traditional qualifications the professional body and the academic community are operating from a relatively common hymn sheet, although this is not always apparent. However, many academics and even representatives of professional bodies are still in total ignorance of NVQs. What is known is based on hearsay, much of it not favourable. Only recently (summer 1995) I came across a senior academic from a well respected university who said that any introduction of NVQs into his institution would be 'over my dead body'.

The problems are further enhanced by the added complexities to the documentation, as one tries to capture in some relatively user-friendly form a representation of how the two types of award are going to relate to each other. It is possible. It has been done. But it is not easy. It requires a lot of sensitivity and sympathy, especially from the chair of the panel and from the university validation officer. It entails substantial advance lobbying and explanation.

Success is certainly more likely if one establishes a good working relationship with the validation officer in advance of the validation event and ensures that she or he is absolutely clear about the programme objectives, philosophy and assessment methodology, and how 'academic' rigour is going to be sustained. In any case it is unlikely that the higher education institution will allow the programme to go

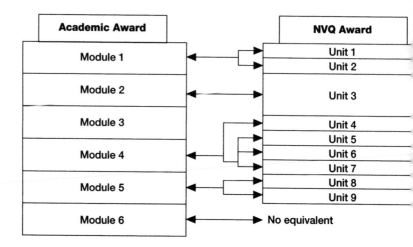

Figure 6.7 Example of the cross-mapping model: mapping for a hybrid awa

forward for external scrutiny unless there is a reasonable degree
comfort with what is being proposed.

Usually, the programme team can nominate their external scruti
eers, who are typically subject experts from similar institutions. If o
is trying to validate a hybrid programme, it is wise to ensure that t
external assessors have considerable sympathy with the ethos
NVQs and, ideally, themselves have some past experience in a
exposure to them.

Question 3

What strategy might be adopted for delivering hybrid programm
spanning the academic–NVQ divide?

For a suggested answer see Chapter 17.

References

1 Debling G. (1995) *Panacea and Parity: Addressing the Myths about NVQs a
SVQs* (*Competence and Assessment No. 29*), Employment Department, Jun
2 Randall J. (1995) *National Vocational Qualifications in Higher Education –
Possible Model* (*Competence and Assessment No. 29*), Employment Depa
ment, June.
3 Walton J. (1994) *Vocational Qualifications at Professional Level* (*Competence a
Assessment No. 26*), Employment Department, July.
4 CVCP (1995) *A Strategy for Vocational Higher Education* (*Competence a
Assessment No. 29*), Employment Department, June.
5 Otter S. (1995) *Higher Level NVQs/SVQs – Their Possible Implications
Higher Education* (*Competence and Assessment No. 29*), Employment Depa
ment, June.

Part Two

Running NVQ Programmes

7 Getting accredited as a licensed provider for an NVQ programme

Objectives

By the end of this chapter you should be able to:

1 Describe the process entailed in becoming a licensed provider.
2 Have a set of criteria for deciding which awarding body to register with.
3 Produce a centre application which will meet awarding body requirements.
4 Prepare yourself for a site-approval visit.
5 Produce a job description for a centre manager.

Introduction

To offer an NVQ programme, providers need to be approved as a designated NVQ centre and registered with an awarding body. It is not the National Council for Vocational Qualifications (NCVQ) that approves the centre. Approval comes from the awarding bodies to whom authority has been delegated.

The first decision that needs to be taken by an intending provider is which awarding body to go for. There are a number of possibilities ranging from the BTEC and the Royal Society for the Encouragement of Arts, Manufacturers and Commerce (RSA) which offer awards covering a range of accredited occupational areas, to more specialist awarding bodies such as the Institute of Personnel and Development, the Institute of Management and the Management Verification Consortium.

It is possible to be approved by more than one awarding body, although that can cause some difficulties if there are different expectations by the awarding bodies. Problems can also occur if the external verifiers allocated to a centre by each awarding body see their role in different lights.

Most awarding bodies have developed guidelines for centres and can be quite welcoming in their literature. Statements I have come across include

We aim to provide a friendly and helpful service to our centres. From the

moment of first registration with us centres are encouraged to ring
write to our staff if they require any advice or assistance.

This handbook explains how we want to work with you to achieve ar
control quality in our qualifications. It also tells you how you can help u
We believe that quality means team work, and that we can only achiev
quality together.

The Institute regards its relationship with centres as a constructive ar
positive partnership.

National guidelines

However welcoming the introductions are, it is important for you
familiarize yourself with the approach of a given awarding bod
Each awarding body will have its own discrete set of systems ar
procedures, but will nevertheless have to comply with the rules of t
NCVQ and the guidelines of the 1993 *Awarding Bodies Common Acco*
(1).

The latest NVQ formulation at the time of writing is the January 19!
NVQ Criteria and Guidance (2). Key statements include:

Applications for approval should be assessed against a common set
criteria including:

- management systems
- physical resources
- staff resources
- assessment
- quality assurance and control
- equal opportunities and access. (2: p. 42)

Each of these headings are covered in the Common Accord, althou₤
the January 1995 NVQ Criteria and Guidance state that they a
provisional and likely to be developed further.

Each centre should receive a copy of the centre approval criteria to guic
its practice . . . The criteria should be the only basis for granting or wit
holding approval. The criteria are a key component of quality assurani
and will be considered as part of the submission process and durir
post-accreditation monitoring.

In the case of a new centre . . . approval should not be granted
the absence of necessary evidence or in the light of contrary evidenc
Instead the prospective centre should be offered further support. Th
approval of a new centre should always ultimately be based on a si

visit to establish liaison and form a proper judgment on whether the centre can meet the approval criteria.

Approval should be granted for a fixed period taking account of the period of NCVQ accreditation of the award. Monitoring is necessary during the period of approval to ensure that the centre continues to meet all criteria. In cases of serious or consistent failure to meet the criteria, approval should always be withdrawn. (2: p. 43)

The NVQ criteria make the important point that approved centres may not automatically extend their boundaries overseas. The awarding body must approve an overseas centre separately.

Specific criteria to be borne in mind if a centre wishes to operate overseas include:

- The need to ensure that quality assurance arrangements of equal rigour are applied.
- The need to ensure that candidates meet the statement of competence in full without varying evidence requirements.
- The need to ensure that, where candidates outside the UK are assessed in a language other than English, the certificate states the language of assessment.
- The cost implications of external verification arrangements.
- The limitations imposed by local requirements for skills, or differences in legal, cultural or technical issues.

The issue of language is further addressed for UK centres, and specific reference is made to centres operating in Wales. The NVQ criteria state that assessment may be carried out entirely in the medium of Welsh, in which case the resulting certificate will note this. Another clause states that units may be conducted in a language other than English, provided that clear evidence is available that the candidate is competent in English to the standard required for competent performance throughout the UK.

Making contact with an awarding body

Typically the following sequence of events occurs:

- The centre contacts an awarding body and receives an information pack including an application form.
- The centre completes the application form, giving details of how their current and intended practices and procedures meet the awarding body centre-approval criteria, and the NVQ qualifications it intends to offer. The BTEC specifically separate out centre-approval and qualification-approval items.

- The awarding body checks through the centre's proposal, and contacts the centre to clarify any queries and omissions.
- Intending centres will be expected to pay a registration fee to the awarding body to cover costs which include the site visit.
- The centre will be notified of the date of the site visit. It could also receive from the awarding body a checklist of points from the completed application form that will be focused on during the visit.

The site visit

The centre will receive a site visit before receiving approval. The visit could be by one individual, typically an external verifier, sent by the awarding body. However, some awarding bodies send a panel of assessors. For example the Institute of Management send a panel to the intending centre. The panel is normally chaired by a member of their Approvals Board and includes an external verifier, a validation officer and other members who might be required to provide specialist input.

The length of the site visit can last from a couple of hours to a full day, depending on issues arising from the original application form and the awarding body's policy. The Institute of Management guidelines state that their panel visit occupies a day, during which each section of the proposal will be considered. The main purpose of the visit is 'to ascertain that the arrangements as described in the proposal will be put into effective operation'.

The Institute of Management guidelines state that a typical programme for a panel visit is as follows.

- Panel assembles at centre.
- Private meeting of panel.
- Panel meets core members of the programme team.
- Tour of centre facilities.
- Lunch with local employers, mentors and potential candidates.
- Private meeting of panel.
- Panel meets full programme team.
- Panel meets senior management of the centre.
- Private meeting of the panel.
- Closing discussion with programme team.

During the visit the panel should meet:

- The internal verifier.
- The programme co-ordinator.
- All members of the programme team (full-and part-time).

In addition, if not included in the above:

- The Principal or Chief Executive, or a deputy.
- The persons responsible for the centre's quality-control systems.
- The librarian and a representative of the information technology facilities.
- Representative employers and mentors.
- A representative of the local Institute of Management branch.

The panel is authorized by the Institute's Approvals Board to inform the centre of the outcome of its visit at the end of the day.

This approach is very similar to the traditional validational event still undergone by many universities seeking to get approval for new programmes.

Preparing the application

It is well worth spending some time thinking through the application form. As with job application forms, a poorly presented form can create a bad impression. The Institute of Management provide detailed advice on the production of a centre proposal which goes beyond the submission of an application form.

Their guidelines state that an application should be presented in similar format to an NVQ/SVQ portfolio and evidence file. Like a user's manual it should provide a detailed breakdown of the operation of the programme. It should be supported by an 'evidence file' which includes sample documents, brochures, diagrams and flow charts, together with CVs of the staff involved with the conduct of the programme. As with candidate portfolios, one piece of evidence may relate to several items in the proposal There should be clear cross-referencing between the proposal and the evidence file.

Before you apply for centre approval you need to ensure that you are capable of offering accreditation of prior learning, development and assessment to candidates from day one of provisional approval being afforded. Accordingly, you must have a 'cadre' of 'competent' advisers, assessors and verifiers in place, holding the relevant D Units of the Training and Development Lead Body (TDLB).

You will need to have in place a centre manager or equivalent. (An example of a job description for a centre manager is given at the end of this chapter.)

You should be able to answer 'yes' or to be able to give full details, as appropriate, to all the questions listed below.

Centre policy

- Do you have an explicit policy for promoting and implementing NVQs Do you have a business plan describing the organization's policy in relation to NVQs?
- Do you have a member of senior management who will formally approve the centre's agreement with the awarding body?
- Is there an action plan for the implementation of the centre's equal opportunities policy?
- Is there an effective appeals procedure for candidates?

Staff resources and responsibilities

- Are NVQ-related roles, responsibilities and authority clearly defined?
- Do you have a job description for the centre co-ordinator/manager?
- Do you have specified procedures for communicating within the NV(team and with senior management?
- Is an NVQ staff development programme in place to ensure that ther are sufficient assessors who are working towards or have already achieved appropriate D Unit accreditation?
- Are there sufficient internal verifiers in place to ensure quality assessments and do these internal verifiers have or are working towards appropriate TDLB D Unit accreditation?
- Are staff-development needs periodically reviewed? Do you have a staff-development plan to demonstrate this?

Information, guidance and advice to candidates

- Do you have sufficient staff available to provide information, advice and counselling for all NVQ candidates? Who are they?
- Do you have information leaflets on NVQs and how candidates migh access assessment?
- How do you ensure that candidates will have full details of the standards? (Some awarding bodies provide as part of the candidate registration fee candidate packs which include full details of the standards.)

Physical resources

- What physical resources are you dedicating to the NVQ provision?
- How will you ensure that any specific resource needs in relation to th NVQ and equal opportunities are made available?
- What mechanism exists for the ongoing review of resources and for ensuring that any deficiencies are identified, prioritized and met?
- Do you have appropriate health and safety arrangements in place in relation to equipment, procedures and accommodation?

Assessment

- How do you propose to ensure that an appropriate range of assessment methods is available?
- What system is in place for co-ordinating assessment?
- What system do you propose for reviewing the quality and fairness of the assessment process?

Records and administration

- What system do you have for recording and updating candidate assessment?
- How will you ensure that records of candidates' registration, achievement and certification are kept up to date?
- How will you monitor candidates' achievements in light of your equal opportunities policy? What records do you propose to keep in respect of data relating to age, gender, ethnicity and disability?

Monitoring and review

- How do you propose to monitor and review the quality of assessment?
- Do you have a system for monitoring and evaluating achievement rates of candidates in relation to equal opportunities?
- How will you identify candidates with special needs and meet their assessment requirements?
- Do you have a review panel which includes, as a minimum, the centre co-ordinator, internal verifiers and assessors and candidate representatives.

Preparing for the site visit

In preparation for the visit, centres are recommended to do the following:

- Brief fully each member of the team about the visit. The team should include not just accredited assessors and verifiers, but also any administrative support required for the programme.
- If the awarding body specify that people outside of the team should be available, such as the site librarian and a senior member of management, ensure that they are familiar with the details of the proposed application.

- Make sure that you have booked a room for the visit. Make sure also that your administrative and record keeping system is available for scrutiny.
- Try to have available portfolios from your assessors and internal verifiers. Some awarding bodies encourage centres to prepare a portfolio of evidence, covering the key criteria referred to in the checklist.

Following approval you will be allocated an external verifier who could well be attached to the centre for the period of initial approval which could range from one to five years. It is most important to establish a good positive working relationship with the external verifier. This is addressed more specifically in Chapter 11.

Example of NVQ Centre Manager job description

POSTHOLDER: NVQ Centre Manager
ACCOUNTABLE TO: NVQ Management Board
SPAN OF ROLE: Co-ordination, integration and development of existing and emerging management, TDLB and other related lead body awards at NVQ levels 3–5, including partnerships and franchises
Responsible for: Centre administration staff, non-academic advisers, assessors and internal verifiers

Responsibilities and authority

A Implement the Business Plan

(i) As agreed with NVQ Management Board and developed in conjunction with the overall strategy of the Centre.
(ii) Establish the NVQ Centre as a self-financing business venture; market the service to create maximum opportunity for the Centre in a competitive environment.

B Continuous Development

1 Initiate and implement change and improvement in services and systems within the NVQ Centre.
    1.1 Identify opportunities for improvement in services and systems affecting the delivery and assessment of NVQs and their integration with academic qualifications.

Evaluate proposed changes for benefits and disadvantages. Negotiate and agree the introduction of change.

1.2 Implement and evaluate changes to services and systems. Introduce, develop and evaluate quality-assurance systems in line with Awarding Body requirements.

2 Monitor, maintain and improve service delivery.

2.1 Establish and maintain the supply of resources into the Centre. Establish and agree customer requirements. Maintain and improve operations against quality and functional specifications. Create and maintain the necessary conditions for productive work.

2.2 Develop processes to ensure the accreditation of Assessors and Verifiers. Develop systems to ensure Awarding Body re-accreditation.

3 Monitor and control the use of resources.
Control costs and enhance value. Monitor and control activities against budgets.

4 Secure effective resource allocation for activities and projects.
Justify proposals for expenditure on projects. Negotiate and agree budgets with NVQ Management Board.

5 Recruit and select personnel.
Define future personnel requirements against Business Plan. Determine specifications to secure quality people. Participate in selection panels to assess and select candidates against Centre requirements.

6 Develop teams, individuals and self to enhance performance.
Develop and improve administration and NVQ teams through planning and relevant activities. Identify, agree, review and improve NVQ related development activities for individuals directly and indirectly servicing the Centre.
Develop self within the job role. Evaluate and improve the development processes used.

7 Plan, allocate and evaluate work carried out by teams, individuals and self.
Carry out performance reviews and appraisals for non-academic staff in order to:

(a) Agree, set and update work objectives for teams and individuals. Plan activities and determine work methods to achieve objectives.

(b) Agree allocation of work and evaluate teams, individuals and self against objectives. Provide and invite feedback from teams and individuals on performance.

8   Create, maintain and enhance effective working relationships. Establish effective relationships with and maintain the trust and support of staff, colleagues, NVQ programme managers, members of the NVQ Management Board, and immediate manager. Identify and minimize interpersonal conflict. Initiate disciplinary and grievance procedures where necessary. Counsel staff. Liaise with External Verifiers and Awarding Body staff responsible for candidate registration and certification arrangements.

9   Seek, evaluate and organize information for action.

Obtain and evaluate information to aid decision-making. Forecast trends and developments which affect objectives. Record and store information.

10   Exchange information to solve problems and make decisions.

Lead meetings and group discussions and make contributions to solve problems and make decisions to meet Awarding Body requirements. Advise and inform others.

References

1   *The Awarding Bodies Common Accord*, NCVQ, August 1993.
2   *NVQ Criteria and Guidance*, NCVQ, January 1995.

8 Valid, reliable and cost-effective assessment at higher levels

Objectives

By the end of this chapter you should be able to:

1 Establish why the provision of cost-effective assessment is becoming of concern in the provision of NVQs.
2 Differentiate between valid and reliable assessment in NVQ terms.
3 Understand how sufficiency and consistency of evidence contribute to validity and reliability.
4 Identify approaches to providing cost-effective assessment, without sacrificing quality.

Introduction

One of the big criticisms associated with NVQs has been the time involvement in, and cost of, assessment. One of the questions asked in the October 1995 *Review of 100 NVQs/SVQs Consultation Document* (1) is: 'How could the costs of assessment be reduced without sacrificing quality?'

This section is concerned with establishing why these criticisms have been voiced, and looking at ways in which the assessment load can be managed by both candidates and assessors at the higher levels. In so doing, it addresses in some detail the assessment philosophy underpinning NVQs.

Debling and Stuart (2), in somewhat defensive mode, suggest that in many traditional vocational qualifications much of the real cost of assessment has been hidden, with remuneration being nominal and not a real reflection of the opportunity costs to those involved. However, Debling and Stuart are thinking of the load on assessors. The issue is not just a function of the burden on them. Of equal, if not greater, concern is the load on candidates who have to provide evidence for assessment. If too much is demanded of them, then it will have detrimental effects on completion rates for a given qualification and reflect badly on the centre, the assessors and the advisors. At lower levels it is less likely that candidates will be responsible for gathering their own evidence for assessment, although views on this are changing.

Mitchell and Sturton (3) summarize a project whose terms of reference were that 'there would seem to be significant scope for improving the cost-effectiveness of NVQ assessment by shifting more of the evidence collection and review within the assessment process on to the candidate'. At higher levels there is a strong expectation that candidates will take significant responsibility for the process; there are repeated references in the literature to the candidate's role in putting together a portfolio of evidence.

In this sense one can readily see how the workload can seem to be greater than with traditional qualifications where students are typically given a finite number of assignments to be undertaken over a course of study, plus a final examination. Indeed, many university programmes now limit the number of assignments to two per unit of study undertaken. Thus for a typical two-year programme leading to a postgraduate diploma there will be seven or eight units and fourteen to sixteen assessments.

It is not meaningful to compare NVQs with conventional academic approaches and think of them in terms of the number of assessments to be carried out. In extreme cases there may only be one, conducted by the assessor on a candidate's finished portfolio, and then subject to internal and external verification. What is significant has nothing to do with such traditional qualification concerns such as how many pieces of work are set and submitted. Rather it has to do with the provision of sufficient evidence by candidates to allow competence to be inferred. To achieve an NVQ *every* performance criterion of *every* element of competence of *every* unit which makes up a qualification should be demonstrated to the standard required for employment – irrespective of how many pieces and types of evidence are involved. The overriding issue is how and where can boundaries be established so that the task does not become endless.

At one stage a number of assessors interpreted the rules in such a way that they were asking candidates for separate evidence against every performance criterion. Various directives from the National Council for Vocational Qualifications (NCVQ) have indicated that this is a faulty interpretation, and that integrative forms of evidence are encouraged. Clearly, the fewer pieces of evidence that need to be provided, the easier it is likely to be for both candidate and assessor.

The judging and deciding aspects of NVQ assessment

As we have seen in previous chapters, the NCVQ guidelines for assessment and verification differentiate between the judging and deciding aspects of assessment.

Judging entails two key aspects:

- *Authenticity* – is the evidence being presented really a candidate's own work or contribution?
- *Validity* – is the evidence being presented for assessment really

relevant to the elements being assessed and in line with the evidence requirements? Is it to the national standards? Are all the relevant performance criteria met?

Deciding also consists of two key aspects:

- *Consistency* – does the evidence show that the candidate consistently meets the standard under workplace conditions rather than showing a one-off demonstration to the standards?
- *Sufficiency* – do the combinations of performance and supporting evidence cover the full range of all the performance criteria, including the contingencies? Do they meet all the evidence requirements?

If one is not careful these requirements can be extremely demanding in terms of volume of evidence. To demonstrate and assess that there is 'sufficient valid evidence' for every element and associated performance criterion can be an extremely time-consuming and daunting task, especially given the associated principle of 'consistency'. A number of suggestions for reducing the load and making it more manageable are made towards the end of this chapter. First we will explore in some detail these underpinning assessment principles.

Validity, reliability and authenticity of assessment

Validity

Validity of assessment is referred to as a principle, by NVQ guides, without being defined. The simplest definition of 'validity' is 'measuring what ought to be measured, or, in this context, assessing what ought to be assessed'.

Johnson and Blinkhorn (4) provide a more sophisticated definition. They suggest that the definition of validity which is most suitable in the context of NVQs is:

. . . the extent to which an assessment process *satisfies the requirements of its own rationale* where the rationale is defined by the core claims of:

- able to perform in a specified range of work related activities to a minimum specified standard
- able to cope with new working methods, employment patterns and practices in so far as these can be foreseen
- able to transfer their skills from place to place and context to context (within reason)
- able to progress to higher NVQ levels more readily than non-competent individuals.

The basis of these 'core claims' was the 1989 NCVQ rubric (*National Vocational Qualifications Criteria and Procedures*) (5). The most current (and more relevant to higher levels) set of 'core claims' is provided by the 1995 *NVQ Criteria and Guidance* (6):

- able to perform to the standards required in employment across a range of circumstances and to meet changing demands
- able to go beyond technical skills and demonstrate skills which include planning, problem solving, dealing with unexpected occurrences, and working with other people
- able to apply the knowledge and understanding that underpins overall competence. (6: p. 5)

Specific reference is also made to the characteristics of a higher level qualification, identifying the following abilities as likely to be demonstrated:

- ability to undertake specialized activities
- ability to transfer competences across a broader range of contexts
- ability to innovate and cope with non-routine activities
- ability to organize and plan work
- ability to supervise others. (6: p. 11)

In essence this entails the assessment of:

- Performance evidence, demonstrating the quality of outcomes of successful performance.
- Evidence of knowledge and understanding from candidates that they are likely to be able to transfer performance to a variety of situations, produce new and creative solutions and deal with the unexpected and the unpredictable

Types of evidence to demonstrate validity

The October 1994 *Place of Knowledge and Understanding in the Development of NVQs and SVQs* (7) identified a number of principles associated with evidence requirements for assessment. Evidence from performance and from knowledge and understanding are both required since each provides a 'unique perspective':

This is because if we wish to infer that individuals are occupationally competent it is necessary to have evidence to show

- they are able to perform the relevant activities to the specified national standard

- they are able to act competently across the range specified
- they have the knowledge and understanding to support that performance. (7: p. 31)

Performance evidence

It is a basic tenet of NVQs that, wherever possible, evidence should be drawn from naturally occurring conditions in the workplace. The more one relies on alternative sources the less likely can it be demonstrated that one is 'assessing what one ought to be assessing'.

However, it has always been recognized that 'simulations' and other specially set tasks might need to be used in circumstances where, for example, performance evidence from the workplace is not available for a given candidate because it is not part of their role.

Knowledge-and-understanding evidence

Knowledge-and-understanding evidence used to be seen as supplementary forms of evidence. Black (8) considered that the combination of workplace assessment and assessment of performance on specially set tasks would often yield sufficient valid evidence to dispense with the need for a separate knowledge-and-understanding assessment. However, the NVQ guidelines have now changed, with a requirement that knowledge-and-understanding specifications be attached to each element in the standards.

While recognizing and appreciating the importance of assessing knowledge and understanding, it adds to the assessor's workload, especially since knowledge and understanding could include, again following the *NCVQ Briefing Series No. 10* (7):

- *Knowing what* – what has to be done in broad or general functional terms and under what circumstances; what information is needed and where to find it; what is meant by it and what to expect; who to contact; when to do something.
- *Knowing how* – how to carry out or perform activities; how something works; how to keep things going; how to manage a number of things at once.
- *Knowing why* – why things are done; the rationale or theory underpinning operations, services, procedures or actions; why a method works or will not work; why things happen; the consequences of failures and omissions. (7: p. 21)

A veritable epistemology! Each of these forms of 'knowing' impose different considerations and demands on the assessor.

Reliability

Reliability is not isolated as a term in the 1994 NVQ Assessment and Verification Guidelines (9). However, the 1995 Criteria and Guidelines (6) state that an NVQ must be: 'awarded on the basis of valid and reliable assessment which ensures that performance to the national standards can be achieved at work' (6: p. 7).

Reliability is made up of a number of ingredients. *Authenticity* is a function of reliability – i.e. can evidence be reliably attributed to a given candidate? *Consistency* is also a function of reliability. Asking the question of whether a candidate will perform to the same standards at a different time and different place is asking for evidence of replicability.

However, there is another aspect to reliability. This is the extent to which different assessors would reach the same judgment about a given candidate's evidence. This is the issue about the extent to which the standards of a qualification are being consistently applied. It accounts for the need to have a number of people involved in an assessment decision, recognizing the fact that the greater the number of people involved, the more expensive the process becomes. The people involved in NVQ assessment are:

- An assessor.
- An internal verifier.
- An external verifier.

In some ways this is not too dissimilar to awards where candidates' work is automatically second-marked. At London Guildhall University, for reliability all assignments must be second-marked and made available for scrutiny by an external examiner. However, not all universities are so rigorous as to demand second-marking of work, which is a very time-consuming process.

It is worth noting that there has been some anxiety expressed nationally about the reliability of the NVQ assessment process. One of the objectives of the group reviewing the 100 most used NVQs was: 'to examine how external assessment might be included in NVQs/ SVQs' (1). Such external assessment would be outside the external verifier system.

Sufficiency and consistency

In NVQs and SVQs a key concern is to obtain sufficient evidence for a safe inference of an individual's competence to be made against the standards, and much has been written on this subject. Note that insufficient evidence is one of the permitted reasons for a candidate not to be given an award.

The NVQ rubric has always set great store by sufficiency of evidence:

An assessment decision must be made as to whether the overall evidence provided demonstrates that the candidate is competent as defined in each element. There must be sufficient, consistent evidence to justify this decision. (6: p. 29)

The notion of 'consistency' is further developed in the same publication:

Candidates must meet all performance criteria consistently, and cover the full range of circumstances in which the competence must be applied, as specified in the range statements. (6: p. 29)

Black (8) identifies three characteristics of sufficiency. To be sufficient evidence must:

* Be sufficiently comprehensive to cover all performance criteria and each component of the range.
* Be available in sufficient quantity to make a good sound judgment.
* Be of a quality which will ensure validity and reliability.

Black argues that an important aspect of sufficiency which is left to practitioners' judgment is that of 'quality'. Evidence will never be sufficient evidence unless it is 'good' evidence.

Another aspect of sufficiency is that of quantity. How much evidence is required. Black feels that if an assessor is confident from having gathered an 'agreed minimum amount of evidence' about an individual that he or she has displayed sufficient evidence of competence to 'pass', there is no need to go on collecting further evidence about that individual. But for other candidates the issue of competence may still be in doubt. 'Sound assessment of competence is more likely than not to result in quite different amounts of evidence being gathered on each candidate'.

Cost-effective assessment

Black (8) argues that decisions about time, cost and practicability of assessment may not have the same gravitas as assessment theory, but are as least as important in determining what can or cannot be achieved.

Debling and Stuart (2) in developing this theme asked the question: 'How can one keep assessment costs down whilst maintaining quality (i.e. ensuring sufficiency of evidence)?'. This is very similar to the question quoted at the beginning of the section from the October 1995 consultation document on the review of 100 S/NVQs.

Debling and Stuart state that most would agree that assessments should do what they are designed to do as economically as possible. This leads them to ask how precise the assessments need to be, given that generally the higher the level of precision sought the greater the cost. They do not answer the question of how precise the assessment should be, arguing that it will vary both between occupational areas and across roles within an occupational area. They go on to suggest that the scale of investment in assessments for a particular occupational area should reflect:

* The value of avoiding, or at least reducing, the probability of critical failure in role performance.
* The potential for that occupational area to contribute to improvements in organizational productivity.
* The potential for that area to contribute to cost reduction.

These themes are not pursued or developed. From the assessor's point of view, only the first criterion would seem to be of concern in terms of the relationship with a given candidate.

Their second and third criteria seem to be employment concerns, not assessment issues. They could be a factor for an employer-based NVQ centre as opposed to an open centre, although this would imply that different candidates are being subjected to different degrees of rigour in assessment. With regard to the point they make about 'scale of investment in assessments', there has been little evidence of awarding bodies providing additional resources to assessors across occupational areas.

Black (8) contends that any number of sophisticated devices can be offered to improve the amount and quality of evidence available for assessment. However, assessment takes place in the real world, where resources and time are limited. Sufficiency thus becomes a balance between certainty and cost.

Thus certain considerations have to be taken into account, including:

* The real amount of time which assessors and employers feel willing and able to make available.
* The extent to which the costs of the solution will be seen as providing good value for money.

Some readers might have a slight feeling of discomfort from the above, that assessment could be reduced to a merely commercial imperative. I would prefer the emphasis to be on what is possible and reasonable given the need to protect the integrity of the qualification afforded.

From the assessor's point of view, Debling and Stuart consider that workload can be reduced by the following measures whilst still meeting overall quality criteria.

sing the outcomes of continuous assessment

Debling and Stuart (2) contend that, if a tutor or supervisor can confirm the authenticity and sufficiency of evidence by means of continuous assessment, this can simplify the task of the assessor. My experience is that this can be particularly helpful when one has candidates on a programme of learning who one sees on a regular basis – say one day a week over a year on an input-driven day release programme. There are certain standards, such as working with others, to which one can attest. One can also request that candidates bring in products from the workplace during the course of a programme which will contribute to the overall assessment. The more that collection and assessment of evidence can be spread out, the more the final load is reduced. (Not necessarily for the internal or external verifier, who will have to rely on the judgement and comments of the internal assessors.)

ncouraging the learner to collect evidence

Particularly at the higher levels, Debling and Stuart (2) suggest that candidates should be responsible for packaging the evidence and presenting it in a form accessible to the assessor. Candidates thus exercise their judgement as to how much evidence is sufficient. Central here is the role of the accreditation of prior learning (APL) advisor. Candidates can be encouraged to provide product evidence such as reports which cover a range of elements and even units. The assessor still needs to cross-map this evidence against the range statements and performance criteria. Again, to do this comprehensively from a portfolio at the end is a daunting task. However, to get candidates to produce piecemeal interim portfolios does not take advantage of the integrative nature of much product evidence; again, a case for a work visit if possible.

Debling and Stuart (2) also emphasize that NVQs are about the assessment of competence in 'whole work' roles. Thus an assessment that 'atomizes' the collection of evidence, and is focused on individual performance criteria, is unlikely to capture the full breadth of competence. Performance criteria provide reference points for making judgements about competence – assessment decisions are a matter of judgement by the assessor about whether the defined standards have been met and whether the evidence is sufficient.

ints for cost-effective and valid assessment

1 Encourage candidates to bring in product evidence of work they have already done relating to specific standards so that it can be 'signed off'. For example for management standards, candidates can bring in

examples of budgets they have been responsible for, with narrativ explanatory accounts of their role in the process.

2   Provide integrative assignments which encourage candidates t demonstrate knowledge and understanding of principles and theorie in support of product and other evidence, e.g. one of SBU integratin assignments.

3   Conduct a work visit towards the end of a programme to reduc the amount of information to be included in the final portfolio (se Chapter 15).

4   Encourage some peer assessment where candidates are engage in an associated programme of learning and are working together fc blocks of time.

5   Identify any 'generic standards' which are covered by virtue c attending a programme of learning. These can be held to be demoi strated by candidates on the basis of observed behaviour during th programme, without the need for them to generate additional portfoli evidence.

References

1 *Review of 100 NVQs/SVQs, Consultation Document*, Evaluation Adviso Group, October 1995.
2 Debling G. and Stuart D. (1992) *Analysing and Minimising the Cost Assessment* (*Competence and Assessment No. 18*), Employment Department.
3 Mitchell M. and Sturton J. (1993) *Doing to or Working With? The Candidate Role in Assessment* (*Competence and Assessment No. 21*), Employme Department.
4 Johnson C. and Blinkhorn J. (1992) *Validating NVQ Assessment* (*Competen and Assessment No. 20*), Employment Department.
5 *National Vocational Qualifications Criteria and Procedures*, NCVQ, 1989.
6 *NVQ Criteria and Guidance*, NCVQ, January 1995.
7 *Place of Knowledge and Understanding in the Development of NVQs and SVC* (*NCVQ Briefing Series No. 10*), NCVQ, October 1994.
8 Black H. (1992) *Sufficiency of Evidence* (*Competence and Assessment No. 20* Employment Department.
9 *Implementing the National Standards for Assessment and Verification*, NCVC February 1994.

9 Becoming an accredited assessor

Objectives

By the end of this chapter you should be able to:

1 Describe the main features of the National Assessor Awards (D 32 and D33).
2 Understand the process you will need to undertake to achieve D32 and D33.
3 For a given element (D321) have an in-depth understanding of what is entailed to meet the evidence requirements.

Introduction

One of the key differences between traditional academic and professional qualifications on the one hand and NVQ qualifications on the other is the requirement that NVQ assessors be accredited to assess. In other words, they need to obtain the appropriate National Standards for Assessment and Verification, popularly known as the Training and Development Lead Body (TDLB) D Units. The two key units for assessors are:

- D32: Assess candidate performance.
- D33: Assess candidates using different sources of evidence.

D32 has four elements, while D33 has three. The key difference between D32 and D33 is that D33 requires you to demonstrate competence as an assessor for at least three candidates, whereas D32 is limited to one candidate.

In the higher education and university sector it can be quite difficult to get lecturers sufficiently motivated to become accredited assessors. Part of the reason for this is that collecting evidence can be deceptively time-consuming. Another reason is that the university reward system doesn't really recognize achievement in becoming an NVQ assessor in the same way as, for example, it recognizes gaining a doctorate or obtaining research funding. Nor are there many universities which provide remission from teaching to become accredited, as they often do for more established qualifications.

In many ways it is quite difficult for university lecturers to get into

the mind set that they need to be accredited as an assessor. Many fee
that they have been involved in assessment for years and that this is ar
unnecessary exercise. However, there is no doubt that those indi
viduals who have gone to the trouble to become assessors have benefit
ted from the process and have looked on assessment in a different light

Background to the D Units

The D Units were first introduced in 1991 as part of the TDLB stand
ards. The intention was that once the NVQ system was fully estab
lished all assessors would possess D32 and D33. Because of criticisms
from the field over the language used in the original standards, they
were rewritten and relaunched in August 1994. At the time of writing i
is still not an absolute requirement that NVQ assessors possess D3.
and D33. The January 1995 *NVQ Criteria and Guidance* (1) merely state
that the eventual target is that assessors possess them. This caveat i
mainly to incorporate the fact that as new standards from new leac
bodies come on board, there will inevitably be a catching-up period
Awarding bodies dealing with established NVQs will expect centres t
have an appropriate complement of accredited assessors.

Current guidelines

In September 1993 an Assessor and Verifier Working Group wa
formed and in February 1994, after consultation with the awarding
bodies, they produced a set of guidelines entitled *Implementing the
National Standards for Assessment and Verification* (2). These should b
read in conjunction with the August 1994 revised *National Standards fo
Assessment and Verification* (3). It would be helpful if you had a copy
of the latter publication with you when reading this section.

Those en route to becoming an assessor should, according to the
guidance notes contained within these guidelines, be designated a
'assessor-candidates'. This, it is claimed, avoids confusion with the
term 'candidates', who are the individuals being assessed by the
assessor-candidate.

Nevertheless, it can still be bewildering to an uninitiated audienc
when it is explained to them that the process may entail an accreditec
assessor assessing an assessor-candidate who is in turn assessing
candidate. This is compounded if the candidate who an assessor
candidate is assessing is another 'assessor-candidate', which in my
experience this can be quite a common occurrence.

The four key stages of the assessment process

The February 1994 Guidance Notes (2) state that the elements of D32 and D33 are based on four key stages in the assessment process which often overlap in practice. These are:

- *Planning* the assessment with the candidate to provide the most effective combinations to suit the candidate.
- *Collecting/collating* performance and supporting evidence.
- *Judging* each combination of performance and supporting evidence based on its authenticity and validity:
  (a) *Authenticity* – is it really a candidate's own work or contribution?
  (b) *Validity* – is it really relevant to the elements being assessed and in line with the evidence requirements? Is it to the national standard? Are all the relevant performance criteria met?
- *Deciding* whether the evidence provided overall demonstrates that the candidate is competent, based on its consistency and sufficiency:
  (a) *Consistency* – does the evidence show that the candidate consistently meets the standard under workplace conditions, rather than showing a one-off demonstration to the standard?
  (b) *Sufficiency* – do the combinations of performance and supporting evidence cover the full range and all the performance criteria, including the contingencies? Do they meet all the evidence requirements?

How the four stages are manifested in the elements of D32 and D33 is shown below:

D32   Assess candidate performance
- Element D321   Agree and review a plan for assessing performance.
- Element D322   Collect and judge performance evidence against criteria.
- Element D323   Collect and judge knowledge evidence.
- Element D324   Make assessment decisions and provide feedback.

D33   Assess candidates using different sources of evidence
- Element D331   Agree and review an assessment plan.
- Element D332   Judge evidence and provide feedback.
- Element D333   Make assessment decisions using differing sources of evidence and provide feedback.

Routes to accreditation

The Guidance Notes go on to state that, in order to maximize acces for all candidates who can meet the required standard, a variety o routes to suit different circumstances need to be available. Assesso candidates who already have substantial experience of S/NVG assessment are likely to need an assessment-only route so that the can achieve the units without having to attend unnecessary trainin However, assessor-candidates with little experience of NVQ asses ment may welcome a programme which covers not only assessme but also identifies developmental needs addressed through trainin courses, supported open-learning, etc.

Assessor-candidates need to check with centres what routes t accreditation are available. The Guidance Notes state that centre should make it absolutely clear what routes are available and also wh is included in the price they are quoting.

Problems of finding candidates

One of the difficulties many would-be assessors have is finding cand dates whom they can assess. In both the further and higher educatio environments, there is a lot of experience in terms of assessing fc qualifications. But it is important that the NVQ assessor-candidate know how to assess for NVQ qualifications with their distinctiv features. Accordingly, it is an NVQ requirement that the would-b assessors' candidates need themselves to be attempting an NVG qualification.

The February 1994 Guidance Notes state that within their 'packag of evidence, assessor-candidates for D32 or D33 must demonstrate th they can assess accurately against national standards. They go on to sa that best practice expects that performance evidence will be provide directly from assessing NVQ-related awards, and that where these ar not yet available, drafts or pilot versions recognized by the Employ ment Department may be used.

Exceptionally, if national standards do not yet exist within th assessor-candidate's area of occupational expertise, some performanc evidence would be accepted from other standards if formatted in ou come terms related to that of existing national standards. Howeve it is, in my opinion, not likely that there will be much deman from assessor-candidates in this category, except perhaps in Scotlanc where outcome-based qualifications in the required format exist mor widely.

D Unit role descriptors

The original Assessor and Verifier Awards provided a role descriptor for each of the D Units and differentiated between first- and second-line assessors

D32 was originally defined as providing standards for a 'first line assessor' or 'workplace assessor' who would normally be a supervisor or manager in the workplace, the trainer in a workshop, a college tutor or a school teacher. The 1991 ITD *Assessor and Verifier Award* booklet (4) suggested that essentially this would be someone who was in daily contact with the individual being assessed and could therefore assess on a continuous basis. The original 1991 D32 Unit guide assumed that assessment would take place 'locally', primarily through observation of performance and examination of the outcomes of such performance, supported by questioning to assess underpinning knowledge and understanding. 'Locally' is a delightfully opaque phrase which is open to many interpretations.

The 1994 formulation no longer refers to 'workplace assessor' or 'first-line assessor'. Instead the unit: 'specifies what has to be achieved by someone making assessments of a candidate's performance under realistic conditions in the workplace, in a training centre or a college' (3: p. 1).

There is some ambiguity in this as to whether the assessor-candidate actually needs to conduct an assessment 'in the workplace'. The section in the February 1994 Guidance Notes which deals with deciding whether the evidence produced overall demonstrates that a candidate is competent, suggests that the candidate consistently needs to meet the standard under 'workplace conditions'.

My reading of the later, August 1994, Guidance Notes (3) is that assessment in 'a college' would suffice. In other words, candidates can bring their evidence (reports, etc.) of what they have done in the workplace to you for assessment purposes, and this would be sufficient. I think this is a pity, and the later section on workplace assessment will develop a case for the work visit for higher level awards. The emphasis is, however, still very much on performance evidence, as the unit title implies.

D33 as originally formulated in 1991 was designed for the 'second-line assessor' who will need to draw upon a wide range of sources of evidence in making the assessment decision. These sources will include judgments made by other assessors, candidate and peer reports, candidate prior achievements and 'direct' assessment as detailed in Unit D32. The 1994 introduction to D33 is similar in tone, but loses the reference to 'second-line assessors'.

In practice it makes more sense, if you have the choice, to go for D33, since by completing that unit you will have covered almost all of D32. This is signalled in the guidance notes for assessors, where it is stated that evidence from the elements making up D33 can contribute to D32. However, you will need to find at least three candidates.

Both D32 and D33 are role-specific, in the sense that there is a clear correlation between the elements, the performance criteria and supporting knowledge evidence, and what assessors have to do. However, the units need a lot of interpretation for someone who is not familiar with 'NVQ-speak'. We will go in some detail through one or two elements to give a flavour of what is entailed. Be warned! The units are not particularly user-friendly and contain a number of oddities and apparent inconsistencies. Because of this, there is also a risk that different awarding bodies, assessment centres and assessors will give contradictory information as to what is required to achieve the units.

You may be able to claim some accreditation of prior learning (APL) if you have been involved in assessment in the past. The February 1994 Guidance Notes state that operating examinations could be accepted as proof of understanding such aspects of pre-set tests as keeping to time, security, confidentiality, etc., which could act as supporting evidence towards D322 and D323.

Similarly, if you can show past arrangements you have made to open access to qualifications for candidates with different special assessment needs, this could be used towards D323, D331 and D341.

The Guidance Notes suggest that such supporting evidence would need to be checked with the awarding body by the external verifier. This seems a tedious and unwieldy process. Check with your assessor as to how amenable he or she is to various forms of supporting evidence, recognizing that there is a remote possibility that these could be challenged at a later stage in the verification process.

D Unit assessment portfolios

To obtain your D32 or D33 you will need to put together a portfolio of evidence. (For more detail on portfolios see Chapter 14.) In general terms, the February 1994 Guidance Notes state that your portfolio of evidence for D32 or D33 should include:

- Copies of assessment plans.
- Records of assessments you have made of candidates' competence.
- Copies of feed-back sheets from your candidates.
- Copies of all assessment records made by your assessor of your competence such as:
  (a) observations of feedback sessions between you and your candidate,
  (b) your assessor's judgements of assessment plans prepared by you,
  (c) your replies to questions demonstrating knowledge.

However, training notes, lesson plans, long descriptive essays and details of why you wish to achieve the units are not relevant.

Although long, descriptive essays are not appropriate; short, contextualizing narrative accounts explaining the evidence and what you have done can be very helpful and I have always encouraged these as an assessor.

Example of narrative account

Report on support and assessment process used with Alison H.

On Tuesday 8 June 1993 I received detailed guidance and guidelines from an external accredited consultant on how to draw up an assessment plan with a candidate for the elements comprising TDLB Unit D33 and also on how to subsequently assess against this assessment plan.

During the day I worked with Alison H., a candidate for D33, and gave her guidance on how she might put together an assessment plan for elements D331 to D333 inclusive. We discussed the types of evidence she would need to include to ensure that she met all the performance criteria and range statements. I emphasized that she would need to provide agreed assessment plans for three candidates she was assessing for an NVQ award. We cross-referred to the Awarding Body Assessor and Verifier booklet to ensure that we were sufficiently comprehensive in our coverage of evidence requirements. I endeavoured to answer the questions and uncertainties that she expressed.

We then met later to look in more detail at the assessment plan which she had developed. We agreed on those areas she would generate evidence for and those areas I would pursue by questioning. I emphasized that I would ask for clarification on any item in her portfolio of evidence which I felt needed expansion. She was aware that the range of assessment options I had available were 'competent', 'insufficient evidence', and 'not yet competent'. I tried to engender an atmosphere of trust and support and to infer that the questions that I would ask would help her to demonstrate that she had adequately covered the whole range. I received from her at the end of our meeting a copy of her assessment plan which we had jointly agreed. We agreed to conduct the final assessment interview on Tuesday June 22 1993.

We will now go in some detail through an element from D32 in order to get a flavour of what is required. Remember that D32 is only asking for evidence from one candidate.

Element D321 agree and review a plan for assessing performance

Unless you are 'in the know', it is impossible to work out from the element what 'a plan' actually is. The performance evidence requirements say that it is an 'assessment plan for one candidate', which takes us a little further but is still not particularly helpful.

Basically what this element is asking you to do is to help a candidate for an NVQ award put together a plan indicating how they are going to demonstrate appropriate performance evidence for assessment. The evidence should be for at least three elements of the NVQ award which the candidate is seeking. The elements may be in the same or different units of competence.

The February 1994 Guidance Notes (2) amplify our understanding of assessment planning. They state that it is encouraged with all candidates, including assessor-candidates, in order to:

- Help identify likely opportunities for collecting evidence efficiently, including opportunities for collecting coherent, common evidence applicable to more that one element.
- Involve them more actively wherever possible in their own assessment process without raising barriers to those people for whom such involvement is inappropriate.

Discussions on the assessment plan should include the collection of evidence which occurs 'spontaneously' within the assessor-candidate's normal work. Integrated assessment is also encouraged where an individual piece of evidence can contribute to several elements; this can be difficult for D32.

However, you will soon get into the swing of it because your assessor will expect you to produce your own assessment plan on how you propose to demonstrate competence against the D Units and associated elements you are aiming for!

Your task, as a candidate-assessor is to:

- Give the candidate guidance as to what sort of performance evidence would be appropriate for the elements he or she is seeking.
- Establish with the candidate how the evidence may be obtained.
- Ensure that the resultant assessment plan covers all the performance criteria for the elements in question.

The process as conceived is quite troublesome for assessors of higher NVQ level awards. Many candidates are seeking a complete qualification rather than a piecemeal accumulation of units. To facilitate this, current NVQ guidance is recommending integrative assessments which give opportunities for demonstrating evidence across a range of units. As indicated in Chapter 14, it is easier to start with a piece of evidence and cross-map it against a number of elements and units. Here we are being asked to focus on as few as three elements, and help candidates produce an assessment plan on an element-by-element basis. I don't think this is good practice at the higher levels. The number of assessment plans could become alarmingly large and, in practice, there is no real benefit for candidates in going through such an atomistic process. It is also very time-consuming and, consequently, expensive.

I have come across situations where would-be assessors have claimed to invent assessment plans for candidates to demonstrate they know how the process works, rather than put real-life candidates through a mechanistic process.

I have heard it stated that the process of becoming an assessor doesn't have to reflect what is subsequently done in practice when you have your licence. However, I am not convinced about the argument that one has to go through a particular and time consuming process only subsequently to unlearn.

Having clarified the overall nature of the assessment plan, the next stage is to establish what the performance criteria entail.

The opportunities identified are relevant to the elements to be assessed

This is quite straightforward. As an assessor, you should be happy that the performance evidence which your candidate is proposing to present is appropriate. You will, of course, need to be familiar with the elements your candidate is being assessed against. I would recommend that if you have a candidate going for a complete qualification you choose elements which give opportunities for a range of performance evidence to be demonstrated.

Best use is made of naturally occurring evidence and related questioning

'Naturally occurring evidence' refers to evidence which naturally occurs at the workplace as opposed to evidence which has in some way been contrived for assessment purposes, such as a role-play simulation of an appraisal or disciplinary interview. It is often subdivided into product evidence and activity based evidence.

Product evidence could be documents and reports, as well as physical outcomes of activities such as refurbished buildings.

Activity-based evidence relates to a process as and when it is undertaken, such as a chairing a meeting.

Related questioning refers to the assessor checking with the candidate for clarification on such matters as why an activity was performed in a particular way or a report produced in the way it was.

The range statements make reference to examination of products and observation of process. However, the range statements are not contextualized to any particular performance criterion, and thus observation of process could be covered by observing a simulation, which is another performance criterion that we shall come to.

Opportunities are selected to minimize disruption to normal activity

This criterion is designed to ensure that assessors don't insist on carrying out workplace observations that interfere with the normal running of the workplace.

Opportunities are selected which provide access to fair and reliable assessment

There is a vast array of material on the reliability of assessment, which falls outside the scope of this particular publication. As a general rule it is considered that the closer one can get to natural work-based conditions of performance then the more reliable the assessment is likely to be. The guidance notes on fair assessment refer to ensuring equal access for candidates including those with special assessment requirements. Special assessment requirements are not defined, but would include candidates with disabilities, unemployed candidates and candidates who are not getting support from their employer. It is quite possible that your candidate for this unit will not have any special assessment requirements. Expect to be questioned by the assessor on how you would help a candidate who is in that situation. Consider also including in your portfolio of evidence an example of how you have helped such a candidate in the past.

When simulations are proposed, accurate information and advice is sought about the validity and administration

The Guidance Notes make it clear that the candidate-assessor is not expected to design simulations but only to know who to ask for advice about their validity. It would seem to me that some knowledge about both validity and simulations would be desirable if one is going to gauge the accuracy of the responses and judge whether a particular simulation was appropriate.

There has been some debate in NVQ circles on what constitutes a simulation. The reference to simulations in the glossary of terms at the back of the *National Standards for Assessment and Verification* (3) makes no attempt at a definition which is not particularly helpful! SCOTVEC's 1993 *Guide to Assessment* (5) defines simulation as: 'any structured assessment exercise involving the organization and achievement of a specific task which seeks to reproduce real life situations. Simulations are used where assessment is difficult to carry out (e.g. for safety reasons)'.

At a recent (1994–95) NCVQ-sponsored project on assessment which I was to some extent involved in, it was suggested that simulation should be contrasted to 'naturally occurring evidence' and covered all forms of evidence which were 'generated' or specifically elicited for the purpose of assessment. This would include special projects or assignments which an individual conducted at the workplace. At the time of writing the outcome of this project has not been officially made public. I suspect that the majority of work projects and work-related assignments have not been validated in any technical sense.

The proposed assessment plan is discussed and agreed with the candidate and others who may be affected

This is fairly self-explanatory. Yet in some ways this is the most difficult of the performance criteria for many assessors of higher level awards to meet because of the nature of the qualification structures. Many candidates for such awards are linked to quite a regimented predetermined syllabus programme and are given integrative assignments to undertake. Thus quite a large proportion of the assessments could be predetermined. There should be little difficulty getting these agreed by the candidate, but it would not be sufficient to meet the evidence requirements for D32.

One way round this is to work out an assessment plan with a candidate towards the end of a programme when gaps are present as a result of evidence presented up to that point. I often determine such an assessment plan following a work visit.

If there is disagreement with the proposed assessment plan, options to the candidate are explained clearly and constructively

The Guidance Notes (2) suggest what the next steps might be if there is a disagreement. Those listed are: postponement of the assessment; seeking another assessor; giving the candidate access to advice from a third party; and withdrawal from the assessment process. There is no indication of how your competence of explaining options 'clearly and constructively' to a candidate – who could well be quite animated – might be demonstrated to the satisfaction of your assessor. Most assessors, I think, would opt for a question: What would you do if you were faced with a candidate who rejected the proposed assessment plan?'

The assessment plan specifies the target elements of competence, the types of evidence to be collected, the assessment methods, the timing of assessments and the arrangements for reviewing progress against the plan

> It is fairly clear as to what is meant here. When you are being asked to put your evidence together many assessors will provide you with a predetermined proforma, looking something like the one shown in Figure 9.1. The expectation is that you would produce something similar for your candidates. As mentioned earlier, this approach can prove somewhat unwieldy and mechanistic in practice when candidates are going for whole awards and, at the beginning of a programme, are not sure what the different elements and units really entail. It is unlikely at higher levels that you would produce a plan just for performance evidence (see D33).

Plans are reviewed and updated at agreed times to reflect the candidate's progress within the qualification

> This is also clear as to what is entailed. It can of course delay getting the D32 award if the assessor wants evidence of reviewing and updating over a period of time with a given candidate. You may be able to demonstrate from other arenas that you have competence in reviewing and updating.

D Unit registration

> The following lists the approach recommended by one awarding body and is typical of what is required.
>
> *1 If you are an individual assessor candidate with considerable experience of NVQ assessment you should:*
>
> - Self-assess against the standards.
> - Register for appropriate unit with a centre.
> - Liaise with accredited assessor to establish an assessment plan.
> - Start collecting a portfolio of evidence.
> - Review the progress/assessment of evidence with your assessor (ongoing).
> - Present your final portfolio.
>
> Subsequent stages will be that the assessor, and then the internal verifier, will deem you to be competent (or otherwise) and, with the agreement of the external verifier, a recommendation will be made to the awarding body that you be awarded the unit. You will then be issued with a certificate.

CANDIDATE NAME										
UNIT:										
ELEMENT										
Item of evidence	Provides support in relation to:									Aspect of range covered	Relevance of evidence
	pca	pcb	pcc	pcd	pce	pcf	pcg	pch	pci	pcj		

Figure 9.1 Assessment plan proforma

Portfolio Development Workshop for TDLB Units D31 to D36

Objectives for the day

By the end of the workshop, we hope you will be able to answer the following questions:

● Which D Units do I need in my role?
● Which am I competent in now?
● Can I prove it?
● Do I need any further training, development or experience?
● What's the way forward?

Provisional programme

9.30 a.m.	Start.
Introductions	Why we think we need D Units. What we hope to get out of the workshop.
Background	NVQ awards and accreditation. What are the TDLB D Units? What is an Awarding Body Licensed Centre?
Clarifying the roles of Assessor, Adviser and Verifier	What do each of these roles mean? What role(s) do you think you have? Which D Units do you need?
11.00 a.m.	Coffee.
What evidence do we need? What have we already got?	Types of evidence. Self-assessment exercise. Review.
12.30 - 1.30 p.m.	Lunch.
Personal action planning	Generating evidence and next steps. CVs. Job descriptions. Finding your way around the Awarding Body pack. Forming support groups.
Review of the day. Future sessions.	
4.30 p.m.	Close.

Figure 9.2 An example of a one-day introductory workshop

2   *If you are an individual assessor candidate with little/no experience of NVQ assessment, you should:*

- Draw up a development plan with the centre advisor.
- Attend a briefing session for NVQ assessors.
- Register for the appropriate unit with the centre.
- Attend training courses/embark upon an open-learning programme.
- Liaise with your assessor to establish an assessment plan.
- Subsequent stages as 1 (above).

References

1   *NVQ Criteria and Guidance*, NCVQ, January 1995.
2   *Implementing the National Standards for Assessment and Verification*, NCVQ, February 1994.
3   *National Standards for Assessment and Verification*, Training and Development Lead Body, August 1994.
4   *Assessor and Verifier Award*, ITD, 1991.
5   *Guide to Assessment*, SCOTVEC, 1993.

10 The role of the internal verifier

Objectives

By the end of this chapter you should be able to:

1 Describe the role of the internal verifier.
2 Indicate the different functions which an internal verifier would be expected to undertake.
3 Establish how internal verifiers might advise and support assessors.
4 Demonstrate the importance of record-keeping.
5 Know how to internally verify the assessment process.

Introduction

The role of 'internal verifier' entails taking responsibility for co ordinating the assessment process for one or more NVQ qualifications at a given assessment centre. It also entails liaising with the awarding body. The *NVQ Report No. 13, National Standards for Assessment and Verification* (1), emphasizes the importance of the role in assuring the necessary quality in assessment arrangements at local level.

The functions covered include supporting assessors, co-ordinating the recording of assessments and undertaking internal verification of assessment practice. There may be one or more internal verifiers associated with an approved assessment centre depending on the size and range of qualifications offered. Internal verifiers should have ob tained Training and Development Lead Body (TDLB) Unit D34 which provides a detailed specification of the functions associated with the role. They should also have gained Units D32 and D33, as Unit D34, in clude the functions of supporting and checking on the practices covered in these two Units.

The National Council for Vocational Qualifications (NCVQ) *Award ing Bodies Common Accord* (2) provides additional guidelines. It reiter ates that internal verifiers are responsible for advising assessors and for maintaining the quality of assessment in a centre. It then goes on to say that they are the arbiters of assessment standards and are responsible for confirming, through systematic sampling of assessments, assessor's judgments that candidates are competent. Necessarily, they must be competent assessors themselves. There will be instances where the internal verifier will be required to double up as an assessor; in such instances there should be review by a second independent internal verifier.

The Common Accord goes on to say that for these reasons internal verifiers should hold D32 and D33 certification as well as D34. This, it is argued, is not as onerous as it may appear at first glance. There is considerable overlap in the evidence that is required to demonstrate competence in unit D34 and in units D32 and D33.

The internal verifier must also have relevant qualifications and/or adequate experience in the appropriate occupational sector to enable accurate judgments to be made about candidates' performance in relation to the occupational standards.

Internal verifiers are expected to check assessors' judgments about individual candidates on a sampling basis. The Common Accord guidelines say that, regardless of whether assessors are on a single site or are distributed across a number of sites, an internal verifier can be expected to have verified the work of all allotted assessors between external verifier visits.

The internal verifier role is, in many respects, the linchpin of the NVQ quality-assurance system. It provides the link between the internal development and assessment process and the external verification and awarding process.

To summarize, internal verification consists of three key roles:

- Ensuring there are sufficient qualified assessors to handle the volume of candidates. This includes providing appropriate training programmes.
- Maintaining an appropriate relationship with the awarding body. This includes ensuring that candidates are properly registered, and that records of candidates' achievements are properly fed through to the awarding body.
- To quality-assure the assessments conducted by accredited assessors and ensure that standards are maintained.

These roles are reflected in the three elements which make up TDLB D34 Internally Verify The Assessment Process.

- Element D341 Advise and support assessors.
- Element D342 Maintain and monitor arrangements for processing assessment information.
- Element D343 Verify assessment practice.

Each of these elements will now be looked at in turn.

Element D341   Advise and Support Assessors

The performance criteria associated with the role are:

- Assessors are provided with full, up-to-date awarding body documentation and guidelines.
- Assessors are given accurate advice and support to enable them to identify and meet their training and development needs.
- Accurate advice is provided about the appropriate and efficient use o different types of evidence.
- Assessors are assisted with arrangements for candidates with specia assessment requirements.
- Allocations of assessor responsibilities are clear and match the need of candidates and assessors.
- Accurate up-to-date advice and relevant support is provided to achieve consistency of assessments.

Gealy et al. (3) observe that internal verifiers have a crucial role i encouraging and assisting new internal assessors to enrol on trainin courses at the earliest opportunity. They should provide addition: guidance and support until the new assessors become more confider in their position.

McFarlane (4) states that training of workplace assessors is normall provided by the internal verifier in the centre and lasts between one t three days. A typical programme includes:

- Principles of the competence-based approach to assessment.
- Development of the award.
- Structure of the qualification.
- Terminology.
- Roles and responsibilities of assessors, internal verifiers, central contacts and external verifiers.
- Standards by reference to an assessor's manual involving element-by-element discussion to clarify evidence requirements and assessment methods.

My experience is that such a programme can be compressed. The mo: time-consuming aspect of the training is the subsequent one-to-or coaching entailed in getting individuals to produce a developmer plan – and the subsequent chasing and cajoling of individual assessor to get their evidence together for assessment purposes against D32 an D33. An example of an introductory one-day programme is given at th end of this chapter.

In the university sector, one of the reasons why so much chasing an cajoling is needed is because there is little encouragement and recogn tion given through staff-development processes for lecturers wishin to become accredited NVQ assessors.

Eraut and Cole (5) highlight the specific expertise required of assessors of professionally based competence qualifications and emphasize particular components to be included in assessor and verifier training if quality assurance is to be maintained. In particular, they maintain, assessors are required:

- To know and to understand the profession's system of assessment.
- To interpret its occupational standards in the agreed manner.
- To collect valid and reliable evidence by techniques such as observation, oral questioning and setting of examinations.
- To apply agreed procedures and criteria in making professional judgments of competence.

All these types of expertise are unlikely to be acquired without both training and active membership of a community of assessors.

Note, however, that the internal verifier is not required to train assessors directly, but to make sure that any assessor training that might be needed is provided.

Element D342 Maintain and Monitor Arrangements for Processing Assessment Information

The associated performance criteria are:

- Ensuring that arrangements for monitoring candidate records and processing information meet awarding body requirements and are sufficient to assure quality.
- Candidate records are complete, legible and accurate.
- Candidate records provide accurate and up-to-date information on monitoring candidate progress within the qualification, and the judgments and assessment decisions made.
- Information is stored securely and disclosed only to those who have a right to it.

Gealy et al. (3) suggest that internal verifiers liaise with awarding bodies, largely through the exchange of documentation. They have to not only complete their own documentation, but also to advise and encourage the internal assessors to complete theirs. They spell out the importance of completing records at the time the evidence is collected and judged. It is all too easy for this to be the first area of practice to slip when there are time pressures. Verifiers and assessors may need constant encouragement to realize that good record-keeping is as critical as making accurate assessments.

Note that this element emphasizes the importance of security over documented assessments. There is an implicit anxiety that candidates or others may tamper with files. This problem can be alleviated by requiring candidates to provide their entire portfolio for summative assessment.

Element D343   Verify Assessment Practice

The performance criteria are as follows:

- The eligibility of individuals to practice as assessors is checked against awarding-body criteria.
- Assessment-practice and quality assurance arrangements are monitored in an appropriate proportion of instances to check that they meet awarding-body requirements.
- Assessors are given clear and constructive feedback.
- Judgments of evidence and assessment decisions are sampled regularly against the national standards to check their fairness and accuracy.
- Documentation is complete, accurate and up to date.
- Decision-makers are given clear explanations of the need for improvements in assessment practice.
- Disputes and appeals are referred to the appropriate authority.
- Recommendations for awarding body action to maintain the quality of assessment are presented clearly and promptly to the external verifier.

Gealy et al. (3) provide the following suggestions. Internal verifiers oversee the internal assessors by sampling assessors and countersigning the decision to award competence on an element. In effect the internal verifier guarantees that the evidence collected and judged against the standards is of sufficient quantity and quality to infer competence. This means that there is a second opinion on the evidence at the frontline. This process also enables the awarding body to have greater confidence that the assessments are carried out to the specified standards.

Internal verifiers are not expected to watch over internal assessors every time they collect and judge evidence. Rather, like the assessor they will be seeking to gain evidence that the assessments made meet the criteria laid down. This could be through observing an assessment as it takes place, or through looking at the outcomes of an assessment such as the documentation produced by some of the candidates. A surprising amount of information can be gleaned from such record scrutiny. In practice, the latter is the quickest and most cost-effective way of conducting internal verification and will be the most commonly undertaken for higher level management qualifications.

Karen Mcfarlane of SCOTVEC (4) argues that regular formal and informal meetings are a most successful way of conducting internal verification. They enhance the quality of the assessment process by giving support to assessors in the interpretation of the standards and dealing with queries early on in the process. Issues can be raised and resolution strategies mutually agreed on a continuous basis, as well as ensuring that the internal verifier is able to monitor activity. Meetings focus on interpretations of the standards and the nature of sufficient evidence as well as identifying possible types and sources of high-quality evidence. (She refers to the Master Agenda suggested in Annex 12.2 of the Assessing Work Based Learning II Project report published by SCOTVEC as *Credit Through Workplace Assessment* 1990.)

Gealy et al. (3) also refer to the value of regular meetings with the internal assessors. They see the purpose of the meetings as being to develop further the assessors' and the verifiers' expertise. Such meetings also serve to support and reassure the assessors by enabling them to discuss problems and successes with their colleagues. Typically, an agenda might include:

- A review of assessment conducted since the last meeting.
- An exploration of any technical or administrative issues that have caused difficulties.
- Development exercises such as assessment of case studies using written materials, audio or video recordings, or role plays.

The need to develop a relationship with the external verifier is an important part of the role. Stage manage meetings, etc. Make sure that all assessors know of the external verifier's visit. Alert the administrative staff or whoever is responsible for holding candidates' records. Book a room where candidates' portfolios can be laid out. Notify candidates of the visit of the external verifier. Technically, the external verifier will wish to see the square root of registered candidates' portfolios. Note that the bulk of portfolios makes it difficult to send samples through the post as one might do with assessed assignments and/or examination papers for an external examiner.

Parallels with the role of the course director or course co-ordinator

There are some parallels between the role of internal verifier and that of course director or course co-ordinator in the academic community. Course directors, often with the assistance of course administrators, are responsible for maintaining an up-to-date record of student results/assessments, liaising with external examiners, and making recommendations to examination boards in respect of whether a particular student should or should not receive an award.

However, course directors don't have the managerial responsibilities implied in the internal verifier role. They do not themselves have an responsibility for checking the quality of assessment of course tutors though they may wish to ensure that some assessed work is doub marked. They do not need to be 'qualified' in their role in the sense th the achievement of the D34 entails.

People who have experience of operating as a course director shoul however, be able to incorporate evidence of record-keeping and liaiso with external bodies as part of their portfolio of evidence. On th whole, individuals who have had a course-director role or equivaler find it more troublesome to get D32 and D33 than D34. By the time the have completed the assessor units, they are experienced in puttin together a portfolio, and can build upon their experiences of cours administration.

Example of accreditation process for an internal-verifier candidate with little experience of co-ordinating NVQ assessmer

Most internal verifiers will have experience of putting together a por folio of evidence by virtue of having obtained D32 and D33. Howeve they may have had little experience of co-ordinating NVQ assessmen The following process for getting accredited is typical.

1 Register for Unit D34 with the awarding body.
2 Draw up a development plan with an assessor (some awardin bodies suggest this should be the external verifier).
3 Attend a training course/embark on an open-learning programme.
4 Start collecting a portfolio of evidence.
5 Review progress/assessment of evidence (perhaps by the extern verifier at each visit).
6 Final assessment of portfolio.

Example of introductory narrative account for portfolio

D34 narrative account

D341

Over the last year I have organized and delivered a number of workshops within the university on assessment criteria for NVQ programmes and the process associated with registration and certification for individual units. The workshops focused on specific training needs against individual D Units and advice was given in accordance with awarding-body regulations. As part of the original process of getting us registered as an ADAC I helped to set up a co-ordination process between myself, our administrator and the Institute. The process included organizing a visit of the awarding-body administrator to our Centre, and of our administrator to the awarding body.

As far as our own programme is concerned, I have helped the group distinguish between the various assessor and verifier roles, and have provided guidance and support towards getting individuals accredited.

I have frequently given advice on ways in which additional evidence can be generated against our level-5 programme. This has included advice on the development of integrating assignments, on what to look for on visits to the workplace, and simulations. Special-needs candidates have included individuals whose role is not totally congruent with the standards – I have helped assessors with identifying development opportunities, as mentioned above.

D342

For many years I have operated as liaison between the providing centre and the awarding body on the old pre-NVQ Diploma programme. I have detailed records in respect of each student's registration and progress going back over many years. I took total responsibility for notifying the Institute of initial registration and of examination and other assessment results and arranged for the production of Diplomas. Records were kept securely in my office.

D343

For many years I have operated as a moderator on the old Diploma programme. My portfolio contains evidence of the support I have given to providing centres, the way I have liaised with the Awarding Body, and the way I have handled disputes and appeals. On our current level-5 programme I have assisted the Course Director in developing assessment documentation and in checking via our internal 'exam boards' that such documentation is up to date.

As part of the moderating process I have conducted a range of checks on the assessment quality and practices of a number of assessors (see portfolio). I have also undertaken some checking of the level-5 portfolios of our students and confirming, or otherwise, assessment judgments.

References

1 *National Standards for Assessment and Verification* (*NVQ Report No. 13*), NCVQ, 1992.
2 *NCVQ Awarding Bodies Common Accord*, NCVQ 1993.
3 Gealy. N. et al. Designing assessment systems for national certification, in *Development of Assessable Standards for National Certification* (ed. E. Fennell), Employment Department Group.
4 McFarlane K. (1993) Towards best assessment practice, *Competence and Assessment*, **22**.
5 Eraut. M. and Cole. G. (1993) Assessment of competence in higher level occupations, *Competence and Assessment*, **21**.

11 Relationship between providers and external verifiers/examiners

Objectives

By the end of this chapter you should be able to:

1 Describe the key features of the external verifier role.
2 Compare the role of external verifier with that of external examiner and moderator and identify similarities and differences.
3 Consider the pros and cons of the same individual carrying out the external examiner and verifier role for hybrid qualifications at higher levels.
4 Identify basic approaches to developing a working relationship with your external assessors.

Introduction

The achievement of outcomes which reliably indicate level of attainment by candidates against a notional or explicit set of standards is a requirement of any credible qualification system. The guardians of such standards are the accrediting bodies who provide the final certification and their agents, who can include internal and external assessors of candidates' work.

Accrediting bodies include national bodies such as the BTEC and the City and Guilds. They also include professional bodies such as the Institute of Management, the Institute of Bankers and the Chartered Institute of Secretaries. They also include individual universities which have the right to confer their own degrees at both graduate and postgraduate level.

Internal assessors operate from within the centre where candidates are provided with the learning and development experiences to enable them to submit for a given qualification. They are given delegated authority to mark/grade/judge candidates' work. University lecturers are an example of internal assessors. In NVQ terms, as we have seen, they include both assessors and internal verifiers and each needs to possess the appropriate D Units to demonstrate that they are competent to assess.

External assessors are appointed by the accrediting bodies to confirm recommendations that candidates should receive a given award; additionally, they may be required to police the system and assure quality.

Some external assessors thus have a quality audit role and moderate both candidate outcomes and the process leading to the attainment of such outcomes. Some qualification systems rely only on external assessors to determine outcomes, e.g. GCSE A levels. In NVQ terms such external assessors are called *external verifiers*; universities almost universally use the term *external examiner*. Other common terms are 'moderator' and 'external assessor'. As we shall see, different qualification systems and different awarding bodies expect different things of their externals assessors.

The relationship which is established between the providing centre and the external assessor appointed by the accrediting body is most important for the development and even continuation of a programme, and is the theme of this chapter.

If the relationship does not work, then it is the source of ongoing tensions. Each visit made by the external assessor is seen as a threat. The opportunity for the provider to learn from the external assessor and, accordingly, to develop the programme to their own and candidates' benefit is not taken. In extreme cases there is also a risk that the external assessor will recommend to the accrediting body that the provider's licence be withdrawn.

However, the relationship should not become so cosy that it seems as if the external assessor is purely acting in a rubber-stamping role. Most accrediting bodies build in a safeguard against such a possibility by fixing a time-scale over which a given external assessor can operate with a given provider.

As can be seen from the analysis of the internal-verifier role (Chapter 10), the NVQ framework makes no demands on the provider in terms of quality of delivery of programmes. To recap, the role of the internal-verifier is defined as being key in assuring the necessary quality in assessment arrangements at local level. It includes supporting assessors, co-ordinating the collection of evidence and undertaking internal verification of assessment practice. There may be one or more internal-verifiers associated with an approved assessment centre, depending on the size and range of qualifications offered. In NVQ terms the role is thus restricted to:

- Providing advice and support to assessors.
- Maintaining and submitting assessment documentation.
- Undertaking internal verification (of assessments already conducted).

External verifiers

This logic is continued in the way in which the external verifier role is perceived within the NVQ award structure. External verifiers are normally employed by awarding bodies (the NVQ term for accrediting bodies) to act as their agents.

Origins of term and definition

The term 'external verifier' was introduced to cover the external assessment role within the S/NVQ system and is universally applied. The (November 1992) *Awarding Bodies Common Accord* Consultation Paper (1) states that external verifiers are appointed by the awarding body to provide verification of the quality of assessments and internal quality-assurance arrangements

Purpose of external-verifier system

The publications of the National Council for Vocational Qualifications (NCVQ) emphasize the primacy of quality assurance and maintaining national standards:

NCVQ has an overriding reponsibility for ensuring that awarding bodies have adequate arrangements and resources for quality assurance and that systems approved at the time of accreditation operate effectively. (1: p. 31)

Awarding bodies are responsible for verifying that assessment in an approved centre is carried out systematically, validly, and to national standards. This is achieved through external verifiers appointed by the awarding body. (2: p. 41)

Verification, the process of monitoring assessment, has two main purposes. First, it acts as a check on the competence of assessors and secondly, it forms links between the awarding body and assessors allowing feedback from assessors on aspects of the system. (1: p. 31)

The role of external verifier

The Training and Development Lead Body (TDLB) Assessor and Verifier Award D35 Externally Verify the Assessment Process, describes the national requirements of the external verifier role. It specifies three key elements of the role (3):

- Providing information, advisory and support services for centres.
- Verifying assessment practice and centre procedures.
- Maintaining records of visits and providing feedback to the awarding body.

The NVQ role descriptor states that the external verifier provides a key link in the quality-assurance chain, supporting and advising centres, and monitoring the quality of their assessment process. The role includes advising centres on any improvements that may be needed in order to meet awarding body requirements and reporting back to the awarding body on the overall quality of assessment in each centre.

The *Awarding Bodies Common Accord* (4) states that external verifiers should:

... check the internal systems of the approved centre and also sample assessment practices and decisions. As the main link between the awarding body and the approved centre the external verifier also has to provide support and feedback to the centre. By helping centres to develop their internal quality systems the external verifier assists them in gaining approval, and in a process of continuous improvement. (4: p. 6)

The 1992 consultation document leading to the Common Accord (1) included the following useful guidelines which, interestingly, were mostly excluded from the final version:

• External verifiers need time to develop a detailed understanding of how a centre works, to identify development needs and advice and support.
• External verifiers have the right to interview candidates, talk to assessors and internal verifiers, visit satellite sites and discuss the development of the centre's action plan.
• External verifiers should investigate candidates' records/products and the work of the internal verifier.

The *Awarding Bodies Common Accord* (4) maintained that it was difficult to provide definitive instructions on the number of candidate assessments that an external verifier should sample. Taking into account costs and known examples of good practice, it recommends that the number of candidate records accessed should be the square root of the annual number of those registered, or 10 per cent of candidates, subject to a minimum of five.

There is no reference to monitoring the quality of the learning experience or the content of any learning inputs that might have been provided to candidates. This is reinforced in the recommended content of external verifier reports.

Reports

The *Awarding Body Common Accord* (4) states that external verifiers should: '. . . prepare a report on each centre for which they have responsibility at least annually. The report should be structured so as to comment on the centre's achievements judged against the approval criteria'. The approval criteria are currently under the following headings.

Management systems

1 The centre specifies and maintains an effective system for managing S/NVQs.
2 There are effective administrative arrangements.

Physical resources

1 Sufficient resources are available to assess candidates for S/NVQs.

Staff resources

1 Staff resources are sufficient to deliver assessment for S/NVQs.

Assessment

1 A system for valid and reliable assessment to national standards is specified and maintained.

Quality assurance and control

1 An effective system for quality assurance and control is maintained.

Equal opportunities and access

1 There is clear commitment to equal opportunities.

Skills and competences

The Common Accord states that, ideally, external verifiers should be qualified in TDLB Assessor and Verifier Awards D35, D32 and D33. Additionally, they will all need: '. . . some background which will enable them to judge whether a candidate's performance is meeting the specified standards of occupational competence'. The precise background that would be appropriate, it is contended, will vary between occupational sectors. Thus it is up to the awarding body to specify the precise occupational/sector competence or experience required.

There is an expectation that external verifiers be 'qualified', although the nature of 'qualified' is left open-ended. Nowhere is stated the type or level of qualification required – such as for example the possession of a post-graduate qualification. It would normally be safe to assume that 'qualified' would entail the possession of a qualification at least of the level of those being assessed.

Time involvement

The Common Accord recommends as a baseline two visits a year totalling two days in all for an active centre. In reality, a large centre may require more than this if the role is to be performed effectively.

Training

Training for external verifiers tends, in my experience, to be very good. Not only do verifiers attend programmes to move them towards becoming D Unit accredited, but also many awarding bodies lay on training and briefing events on a fairly regular basis. The importance of awarding bodies providing for the continuing development of their external verifiers is mentioned in the Common Accord (4: p. 10).

Guidelines given by awarding body

Clearly, the guidelines an awarding body gives to its external verifiers about the content of that report is of vital interest to the provider. It gives a clear signal as to the awarding body's philosophy, and a real insight into how the awarding body sees the external verifier's role and responsibilities in carrying out that philosophy.

Some of the awarding bodies have been concerned that the NVQ verification guidelines do not go far enough in terms of quality control and assurance over the student or candidate experience. I recall being involved in a number of debates with an awarding body over the importance of trying to provide some monitoring mechanism over delivery centres who were providing programmes of learning en route to assessment. The argument being put forward in favour of this proposition was that lack of appropriate monitoring could lead to poor-quality providers operating under licence to the awarding body without being detected, and that this in turn would bring the awarding body into disrepute. The counter arguments were that the market would dictate – candidates who were receiving a poor deal would spread the word around and this would, over time make, a 'poor' provider unviable. A second argument that was raised was that if the standard of provision was of a low order then this would affect completion rates. So long as candidate success rates were measured, then one could infer the quality of support that was being given.

However, completion rates for NVQs can be quite slow without any blame being attached to the centre. In particular, it can be quite difficult for candidates to generate evidence across the range of competences.

Different awarding bodies seem to be adopting various approaches to the monitoring arrangements which they are imposing on providers of NVQ awards. The central issue for providers in this is how the awarding bodies see the role of external verifier. Do they restrict the monitoring process to verification of assessment, or do they see their verifiers taking on a more broad-ranging role?

In my opinion, irrespective of how the awarding bodies define their relationship with a provider, the provider has an obligation to develop customer-responsive measures to ensure that there is adequate evaluation of customer satisfaction.

It is interesting to compare the role of external verifier with that of external examiner and moderator, terms which are associated with more established qualification structures. This is particularly significant given the increasing likelihood of hybrid qualifications at higher level which cut across two or more systems. Individuals could end up trying to conduct the joint role of external examiner and external verifier for a given centre.

External examiners

Origins of the term

The term 'external examiner' has been used in the higher education sector for many years to denote such external assessors. Their role has been to ensure the maintainance and enhancement of standards of graduate and post-graduate qualifications awarded by the higher education institutions. The term implies that there will be a terminal examination associated with the qualification and that examination papers will be assessed both internally and externally. The 1989 guidelines for external examiners produced by the committee of Vice Chancellors and Principals (CVCP) of the universities of the UK (5) make that assumption in referring to the external examiner's role in approving draft examination papers and assessing a sample of examination scripts:

The guiding principle for any selection of scripts is that external examiners should have enough evidence to determine that internal marking and classifications are of an appropriate standard and are consistent. (5: p. 6)

Increasingly, university qualifications are being developed in which candidates are continuously assessed without any examination being involved. However, the term 'external examiner' still seems to be universally used.

Some professional bodies and other accrediting bodies have used the term 'external examiner'. Other terms have included 'moderator'. Prior to the introduction of the NVQ system, such roles were based on the academic perspective, and in many cases still are.

Purpose of external-examiner system

According to *Academic Standards in Universities* (5):

. . . the purposes of the external examiner system are to ensure

1   First and most important, that degrees awarded in similar subjects are comparable in standard in different universities in the UK, though their content naturally varies; and
2   Secondly, that the assessment system is fair and is fairly operated in the classification of students.

There is an implicit assumption here that candidates will be graded on some form of scale which differentiates between level of attainment.

External examiner role

The CVCP report goes on to say that, whereas it is 'neither possible nor desirable to establish a uniform external examiner system across all universities and applicable to all subjects' it is desirable that external examiners need to be able:

(a)   to participate in assessment processes for the award of degrees
(b)   to arbitrate or adjudicate on problem cases
(c)   to comment and give advice on course content, balance and structure, on degree schemes, and on assessment processes. (5: p. 4)

In other words, external examiners have a role in both input and output aspects associated with a given qualification. This is reinforced in the recommended content of reports.

Reports

The CVCP paper (5) includes the following guidelines for external examiners' reports:

- Whether the objectives of the course are defined and are appropriate to the subject matter and to the students.
- The course structure and content.
- The assessment process and the schemes for marking and classification.
- The marking standards applied by internal examiners.
- The general quality of candidates' work.
- Comparability with other institutions.

Individual universities often supplement these guidelines. One typically finds reference to:

- Strengths and weaknesses of the students.
- Quality of knowledge and skills demonstrated.
- An expectation that external examiners will have had discussions with students.
- The quality of teaching as indicated by student performance.
- The lessons of assessment for the course curriculum/teaching and learning strategies/staffing and physical resources.

Some professional bodies also provide similar detailed guidance for their external examiners or equivalent. One example is the IPD who state for their report guidelines (6):

- The adequacy of the advance information provided on course structure, content, objectives and assessment.
- Content of the course in terms of academic quality, up-to-dateness of subject matter, development of critical judgment, integration of theory and practice.
- Organization and administration of the course.
- Teaching and learning, including teaching resources and tutor contact with students.
- The functioning of the examination board.
- The extent to which the course team have taken on board the advice and comments of the external examiner.

Skills and competences

The Council for National Academic Awards *CNAA Handbook* (7: Section E3.1) states that to carry out their responsibilities external examiners must be:

- Competent in assessing students' knowledge and skills at higher education level.
- Expert in the field of study concerned.
- Impartial in judgment.
- Properly briefed on their role.

Time commitment

There are no official guidelines on time commitment. In his 1993 analysis, Silver (8) felt that it was not easy to calculate in practice since some of it is scattered in small bursts over the year. Estimates from the field included:

- Hard work for four or five days in advance, and two meetings.
- Three or four days' preparation plus two days' attendance.
- A lot of hard work but it's controllable.

Training

Training for university external examiners is not common beyond issuing instruction papers, regulations, course submissions and report guidelines.

Changing roles of external examiners

Silver (8) started his analysis with the proposition that the external examiner system is under strain, and summarized views emerging from a CNAA-sponsored project into three higher education institutions. He observed that 'there is general recognition that the role of external examiner has changed' in recent years. He quoted one institution as saying 'we have changed the role of the external examiner without rethinking it, and we are now feeling our way forward to understand what the role is to be'. His analysis did not include any reference to changing roles deriving from the emergence of S/NVQs.

Moderator

'Moderator' is a term that has been around for as long as 'external examiner', tends to have a similar meaning, and has long been used by awarding bodies such as the BTEC and by professional bodies for syllabus based programmes. The following extracts from the guidelines of the former Institute of Training and Development (ITD) for moderation of their syllabus-driven programmes are typical:

- Moderation provides the necessary link between providers, their clients and the institute. It is important that an understanding is reached between the moderator and providers about how programmes are delivered, and regarding the necessary candidate support systems and the review and evaluation processes. These should be in line with ITD's criteria for approved providers submission to the Institute.
- The role of the moderator is to advise and assist the provider to improve the quality of provision of its ITD programme(s), as part of the Institute's national quality-assurance system. It is essential that the moderation process begins prior to the start of the programme. This will often require the moderator to take the initiative.
- A moderator's report is to be submitted at the conclusion of each programme, and should include the following:
  (a) specific details of the programme covered by the report,
  (b) number of and reasons for visits to provider,
  (c) extent of involvement in assessment process and results meetings,
  (d) degree to which assessment met the criteria of the Institute,
  (e) programme evaluation, and
  (f) a results list for each participant against the assessment schedule, and a pass list.
- As a guide, moderators should be Corporate Members of the Institute with a training qualification and relevant experience at the level at which they are called upon to moderate. In particular, moderators should:
  (a) be active in the field,
  (b) have professional credibility,
  (c) be up to date on current trends and initiatives in the field,
  (d) be familiar with and understand the Institute's programmes, and
  (e) have detailed knowledge of the programme they are monitoring.

Similarities and differences between roles

The key similarities and differences of the external examiner role in the university system and the external-verifier role are summarized below. In many respects it would be just as applicable to substitute 'professional body' for 'university' and 'moderator' for 'external examiner'.

	External examiners	External verifiers
Who nominates	Course director and vetted imposed by academic standards	Imposed by awarding body
Who appoints	University	NVQ-awarding bodies
Responsible to	University	NVQ-awarding bodies
Tenure	3–4 years	Varied
Criteria	Academic qualification experience in the field	D35 (D32, D33) sector competence
Training	Briefing pack	Awarding body training and ongoing mandatory briefing
Payment	University on production of a written report	Awarding body
Focus	Inputs and outputs	Outputs
Report focus	Academic assessment standards, comparative	Vocational assessment standards
Time needed	Considerable, high percentage not in situ	Considerable, in situ
Focus of assessment	Predominantly knowledge, understanding, conceptual underpinning	Performance evidence packaged in an indexed portfolio
Mental set of role holder	Conceptual sophistication, analysis, synthesis practice grounded in theory, theory grounded in practice	Vocational, practical, competent performance to national standards
Recruitment market	Academics known in their field with practitioner experience	Some academics, but also independent consultants

Motivation	Academic and professional colleague support and part of the merry-go-round	Professional support and income generation
Awarding process	Examination board formal approval by external examiner name by name	No formal approval of individual award by external verifier. No board attendance. Less prescribed

The two roles show some obvious similarities. One core difference is that external verifiers need to be formally accredited as competent in assessment and verification, but only need 'some background' in the area they are assessing. The external examiners, on the other hand, need substantial academic qualifications as well as experience in the field, but are not required to be formally accredited as competent in assessment and verification.

External examiners may be concerned with completion rates and check back against entry requirements and the process onto the programme. External verifiers might be concerned about appropriateness of job role, but not about prior academic attainment.

Perhaps the most significant feature is in the different value structures of the two systems which influences the mind sets of the role-holders.

Advantages of jointly performing the external examiner/external verifier role

The development of NVQ qualifications at levels 4 and 5 has led to the possibility of one individual carrying out the joint role of external examiner for a university award and external verifier for an NVQ award. Until recently, this was the case in the South Bank University programme which led to the simultaneous award of a post-graduate certificate and diploma in human resource development and to NVQ awards at levels 4 and 5 based on TDLB and Management Charter Initiative (MCI) standards.

Such an arrangement has a number of advantages for the provider and for the candidate:

- It means that the candidate's work is subject to only one external

scrutiny and external 'board' and thus simplifies administrative arrangements and makes cost-effective use of time and resources.
- Candidates can be notified of their success, or otherwise, in both awards simultaneously.
- It demonstrates the integrated nature of the qualification and the interaction between post-graduate and NVQ-assessed elements.
- The number of visits by external assessors is reduced.
- The joint-role holder can see all of a candidate's work as being of relevance, as opposed to excluding some aspects of their portfolio as only applicable to one part of the joint qualification.
- Collectively, the joint-role holder can spend more time with a given centre, since both awarding bodies give a separate (and paid) time allowance.

Emerging practical difficulties

1   Simultaneous assessment across two qualification systems embodying different values can create a mind-set conflict which promotes role ambiguity. It has proved very problematic to look at candidates' portfolios and make simultaneous judgments about them from the perspective of how concepts and theories are handled and applied, as required for university post-graduate accreditation, and assessing work-related evidence for competence as required by the S/NVQ awarding body.

External examiners for university and professional awards frequently have to assess practical work related activities and reports. However, this is within the context of a discrete qualification system with its own distinct and internally consistent approach as to how learning is developed and assessed.

2   It leads to a forced choice in focus due to limited time. Which aspect of a candidate's portfolio does one concentrate on? Given a shortage of time, there is a risk that one awarding body's requirements will be given precedence.

3   Linked to the above there is a cognitive overload. It should be recognized in this context that the sheer volume and diversity of information and evidence contained in the portfolios makes the overall assessment process a daunting task, and it is physically and mentally impossible to do justice to all elements.

4   There is also an overload in role expectations. It is worth reflecting that role overload has already been recognized as an issue for individuals operating as 'just' external examiners, without the extra dimension of handling additional external verifier role demands.

Additionally there are a number of general issues that would arise if such an arrangement were to be established as a general rule.

ssues arising

1   A person approved as an external verifier by the NVQ awarding body might not be approved as an external examiner by the university even though the work they are assessing is identical, and vice versa. This situation is quite likely to occur. The NVQ Common Accord guidelines state that external verifiers must have D35, D32 and D33. Additionally, they should also be qualified and/or experienced in the appropriate occupational area. There is no requirement that they hold a post-graduate qualification, which would be a minimum university requirement. Indeed, universities normally are looking for external examiners of post-graduate awards to hold at least a master's qualification. However, universities do not require examiners to have D Units.

The situation with respect to experience in the appropriate occupational area could lead to some contention, and already has done so in a non-NVQ context with respect to joint awards. In social work, for example, some universities are running a joint award in conjunction with The Central Council for the Education and Training of Social Workers (CCETSW). The university award is the Diploma in Higher Education, the CCETSW award is the Diploma in Social Work. The CCETSW has a Register of Approved External Assessors; however, some don't meet university requirements. The situation is not quite like the NVQ external verifier scenario where the awarding body nominates the verifier, although the universities would expect that for a professional qualification there should be some demonstration by examiners of research/consultancy in the relevant field to demonstrate appropriate expertise.

In practice, this is an emerging situation and, given good will on the part of the awarding bodies involved, it should prove possible to identify individuals who would be jointly acceptable.

2   Since the individual is acting as an agent for two bodies, two lots of payment are being made. This might seem a trivial point, but could have implications if one awarding body is paying considerably more than another. There is also the issue as to how one allocates time between awarding bodies.

3   There are differing perceptions between awarding bodies on what constitutes quality of outcomes and what are valid indicators. This can lead to two entirely different reports being written about the same centre's assessments.

4   It could further be the case that a candidate's work is assessed as satisfactory against one set of standards and unsatisfactory (not yet competent) against another. As we have seen there is an inherent tendency for NVQs to look at outcomes which are competence based while universities are concerned with cognitive and theoretical underpinning.

5   External examiners may be concerned with completion rates and

check back against the entry requirements and process wheret individuals get onto a given programme. External verifiers might t concerned about appropriateness of job role, but not about prie academic attainment, except where it is being used to justify a claim fe accreditation of prior learning.

Recommendations for providers

The handling of a joint external examiner/verifier role becomes more workable if:

- The qualification system is conceptualized as two separate co-existing and overlapping systems, i.e. academic–professional and S/NVQ system. The academic-professional system recognizes the importance of work-related assessment, but not at the expense of academic frameworks and theoretical contextualization. The S/NVQ system recognizes the importance of assessing underpinning knowledge and understanding and holistic concept building, but not at the expense of assessing work-placed evidence.
- The potential cognitive dissonance associated with conducting simultaneous assessments for two systems with overlapping but still differing perspectives can be resolved by separating out in time the assessment process.
- Candidates register separately for the post-graduate and the S/NVQ programme, although they should be informed of their interrelationship.
- *All* assessments carried out for the post-graduate award are contextualized against national standards. They will take the form of integrated work-related assignments and projects, and reflective personal-development accounts, as opposed to examinations.
- S/NVQ portfolios incorporate reflective reports/personal-development journals in which candidates explain and justify their actions in generating performance evidence by means of conceptual and theoretical underpinning.
- Candidates are assessed on a sample basis by the external examiner for their post-graduate award on completion of their work-related assignments and projects.
- Candidates' portfolios are assessed by the external verifier as required by the S/NVQ awarding body.

The qualification relationship is illustrated in diagrammatic form in Figure 11.1.

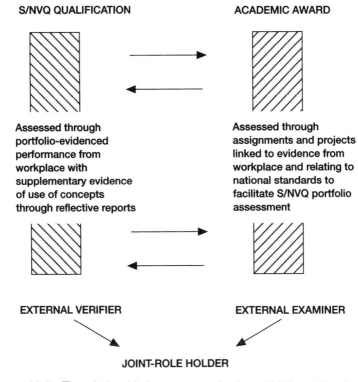

Figure 11.1   The relationship between academic and NVQ qualifications

Other guidelines for providers

- Establish a close and consistent relationship with the external verifier.
- Be absolutely clear as to the guidelines that the awarding bodies set out for verifier and examiner reports.
- Plan visits well in advance. Make sure the documentation is up to date.
- Lay the portfolios out in a systematic way in advance of the visit.
- Ensure that the assessors and course team are available for questioning.
- Ensure that the external verifier is absolutely clear as to the requirements of the university/professional body (if involved in a dual award).
- Clarify with the external verifier what his or her expectations of you are.

Note

In writing this section I am indebted to the advice and guidance and contribution of Barry Baker, Principal Lecturer at Cheltenham and Gloucester College of Higher Education, who has carried out the join role of external examiner and verifier.

References

1 *Awarding Bodies Common Accord, Consultation Version*, NCVQ, November 1992.
2 NVQ Criteria and Guidance, NCVQ, January 1995.
3 *National Standards for Assessment and Verification*, NCVQ, August 1994.
4 *Awarding Bodies Common Accord*, NCVQ, August 1993.
5 *Academic Standards in Universities – a Paper on External Examining in Universities at First Degree and Taught Master's level*, Committee of Vice Chancellors and Principals, 1989.
6 Crosthwaite E. (1994) *External Examiner Guidelines*, IPD.
7 *CNAA Handbook*, 1991–92.
8 Silver H. (1993) *External Examiners: Changing Roles? A Study of Examination Boards, External Examiners and Views of the Future*, CNAA.

12 How to help potential candidates choose an appropriate programme

Objectives

By the end of this chapter you should be able to:

1 Distinguish between the range of programmes offered to candidates, both at centres offering only NVQ programmes and at other centres.
2 Give advice to candidates as to which programme and qualification to aim for.
3 Identify a number of centre support systems to help candidates make appropriate choices.

Introduction

Many candidates for higher level awards have in the past had a very clear picture of the qualification and associated programme/mode of study they are seeking. This is based on word-of-mouth recommendations from previous students/candidates, their reading of the centre's literature, advice from employers, etc.

However, there has always been a high percentage of candidates who apply for programmes/qualifications with either no real understanding of what they are aiming for or not being realistic about what is entailed. Furthermore, a high percentage of enquirers don't follow up their enquiry.

With the development of higher level NVQs, the possibility of higher level GNVQs in the near future, and the development of a spate of professionally oriented master's programmes in recent years, it is likely that potential candidates will be very confused about what is on offer, and will need considerable advice from centres as to what is on offer and how it meets their needs.

Why potential candidates don't register for higher level NVQs

For higher level post-experience programmes, candidates are often seeking a professional qualification and see NVQs as a 'bolt-on' extra. This is because NVQs are still not fully established at the higher levels and many professional bodies either provide alternative qualification routes or no NVQ route at all.

In terms of registering for an NVQ, many candidates are put off fo reasons such as

- Adverse publicity surrounding NVQs.
- Working for organizations with no track record of NVQs.
- Not having a job role which enables them to demonstrate competence at the workplace across a range of units.

Other factors include the following:

1 *The length of time it typically takes to complete an NVQ compared t other qualifications.* Many post-experience qualifications, such as a Cer tificate in Management, are often completed in one year. Experience o NVQs is that the equivalent to a Certificate in Management often take two years. Sunderland University, in a case study reported in an Em ployment Department project in which I was involved (1), found that fo both their Training and Development Lead Body (TDLB) and Manage ment Charter Initiative (MCI) programmes, completion rates over on year were extremely low. The National Council for Vocational Qualifi cations (NCVQ), when approached for advice on this, suggested tha two years was the typical time-scale for completing an S/NVQ qualifi cation. This created problems for Sunderland, given historical comple tion rates for non-NVQ programmes. The experience of South Banl University was that their pilot level 5 TDLB award was completed i eighteen months by 50 per cent of candidates and that all candidate found the learning and development process entailed to be far mor difficult than they had initially bargained for. Interestingly enough completion rates for level 4 TDLB programmes were even lower.

2 *The ambivalent position of some professional bodies towards NVQs, an the existence of alternative, non-NVQ programmes as a route to professiona membership.* NVQs are still being worked through in many professiona bodies to determine whether they are to be awarded equivalent statu to traditional syllabus awards, which show no signs of being replace by NVQs.

3 *Competition from traditional and more established awards.*

Example

A typical example is the Institute of Management (IM). In general, the IM has adopted a very positive approach to NVQ provision and has integrated NVQs into its professional qualification and development route. Thus the IM publicity brochure for their 'Competent Manager Programmes' state that all participants who achieve NVQ level 4 with the IM will automatically qualify for Associate Membership, and those who achieve NVQ level 5 will, with appropriate experience, qualify for the Member grade. The 1994 validation

> document for their in-house Diploma in Management Studies pro-
> vides a range of learning activities for the competence-based
> award, including the production of a portfolio covering the ap-
> propriate MCI competencies. However, there is a caveat that the
> traditional route to management qualifications is likely to maintain
> its current popularity, and that individuals should be provided with
> free access to academic and vocational qualification frameworks.

Nevertheless, the market demand for NVQs can be expected to increase, particularly where candidates come from organizations where
NVQs are recognized and linked to career development and investors
in people.

Choices for intending candidates

At higher levels where NVQs are in existence, individuals have the following choices of post-experience qualifications:

1 *Professional body qualifications,* frequently leading to certificates
and diplomas and often linked to status within the professional body.
These qualifications are often delivered by approved centres who meet
the professional body's quality-assurance requirements.

Many of these professional body qualifications have gained standing
on the university general credit-rating structure affording them a post-
graduate status; thus the IM's Certificate and Diploma in Management
(Competent Management Programme), have been credit-rated by the
Open University Validation Service. The advantage of this to candidates is that it can provide access to university master's programmes,
which are becoming increasingly common.

2 *University and other higher education institutions post-graduate
qualifications,* leading to certificate, diploma and master's awards.
These are often closely linked to professional body requirements.

3 *Higher level NVQs,* still primarily at level 4, although level 5
awards are increasingly coming on-stream.

4 *Hybrid programmes,* which lead to joint NVQ and 'academic'
certification.

5 *Preparatory, pre-competence programmes,* for those whose job roles
do not currently enable them to put together the evidence to achieve an
NVQ award.

Different kinds of centres

We will look at three different types of centre:

- Centres offering NVQ programmes only.
- University centres.
- Non-university centres offering a range of programmes.

Centres offering NVQ programmes only

The decisions for candidates at such centres are

- What level of NVQ to aim at.
- Whether to select an accreditation of prior learning (APL) or programme-based route.
- Which NVQ (i.e. which occupational area/standards).
- Whether to opt for a full qualification or to go for certificated units leading to a qualification.

Level of NVQ to aim at

This depends on an individual candidate's job role and the attitude of the organization for which they work. There are two schools of thought on job role. One perspective is that the individual candidate needs to be in a job role which enables them to generate 'naturally occurring' work-based evidence. However, if someone is currently in a job role which readily allows appropriate work-related evidence to be demonstrated, it could be argued that the qualification is merely an 'endorsement' of what they are currently doing and affords little opportunity for learning or development. This view is hotly contested by those who argue that the task of putting a portfolio of work together is, in itself, developmental. My own view, which reflects that expressed in current NCVQ guidelines, is that, unless the portfolio demonstrates evidence of critical reflection, it is an empty process.

Thus candidates who are operating in a level 3 job role might prefer to aim for a level 4 award, and those at level 4 to aim for level 5, etc., because of the developmental opportunities afforded. This assumes that one is in an organization where the differences between levels can be delineated clearly. This is increasingly less the case, as organizations are 'delayering' and organization roles of even five years ago are changing and/or becoming obsolete. My own experience on the MCI is that in small and medium sized enterprises (SMEs) and, as responsibilities are increasingly delegated to business units, candidates with relatively junior management roles can demonstrate substantial evidence at MCI II.

The attitude of the organization by which the individual is employed could come into consideration. Some organizations encourage individuals to undertake special assigments and projects as part of their development. In the past these have not been undertaken for the purpose of assessment, but to help individuals gain a range of skills for roles they may subsequently move into. Such organizations may well encourage individuals to seek accreditation for such developmental activities.

Other organizations are still hierarchically focused and become defensive if individuals engage in developmental activities, and indeed gain qualifications appropriate to a level higher than that at which they are operating.

However, it should be remembered that the NVQ guidelines emphasize that there should be no artificial restriction to access to a qualification. Thus it is one of the fundamental NVQ criteria that a qualification must be:

- free from barriers which restrict access and progression and available to all those who are able to reach the required standard by whatever means
  and
- take proper account of future needs with regard to technology, markets and employment patterns. (2: p. 5)

APL or programme route

Candidates need to be given advice as to whether to attend a programme of learning or whether to produce their portfolio on the basis of prior achievement.

APL route. In this context, we are talking about accreditation of prior experiential learning (APEL). In extreme cases candidates will endeavour to convince the centre that they:

- Have sufficient knowledge of the NVQ system.
- Have a clear understanding of the particular standards of the qualification they are aimimg at.
- Possess appropriate work-based experience.

In such a case candidates can merely register for a qualification and then get on with putting their portfolio together themselves without any further assistance.

The advantage for the candidate is that this is by far the cheapest option. They are paying merely for an accreditation service. Nevertheless, in nine out of ten cases they will be mistaken in their thinking. There are a lot of misconceptions about APEL. A number of people consider this to be the easy option. As demonstrated in Chapter 14, this is no easy route.

Programme routes. Programme routes fall into two categories. One approach is to provide candidates with detailed information on how to get evidence together, what sort of evidence is appropriate and what is 'sufficient'. There may also be inputs on what the standards aimed at actually mean, an exercise in interpretation and translation. This has proved to be particularly important because the need to compress the standards has often been at the expense of clarity.

The second approach is more closely related to the conventional syllabus model. Knowledge-and-understanding and body-of-knowledge inputs are provided which give a backdrop against which the standards can be contextualized and interpreted. Specific skills development activities can be laid on in order to help candidates generate evidence that might be difficult to carry out in the workplace.

It is not realistic to lay on tailor-made programmes for each candidate, although each candidate is supposed to produce their own development plan with their assessor or advisor.

Depending on candidates' experience they should be directed down one of the three main routes:

- Pure APEL, with no need to attend any input sessions.
- Programme inputs to provide guidance on evidence requirements and standards interpretation.
- Programme inputs on the body of subject-specific knowledge which underpins the standards, together with specific skills development activities.

Some centres may not be large enough to provide programme inputs for this last category and will need to direct candidates to appropriate courses – all of which will add to the costs a candidate will incur. However, this third route is increasingly likely to be required at the higher levels. Hamlin and Stewart (3) have produced the diagram shown in Figure 12.1 to illustrate the increased significance of demonstrating knowledge and understanding at the higher levels. In my opinion their model could usefully be extended (Figure 12.2) to incorporate the need to demonstrate what theories and conceptual understanding have informed candidate's actions.

Which NVQ?

Most centres will only be offering a limited number of NVQs from the range that is on offer. Even given these constraints, there are opportunities for candidate choices. Take, for example, a training manager. He can

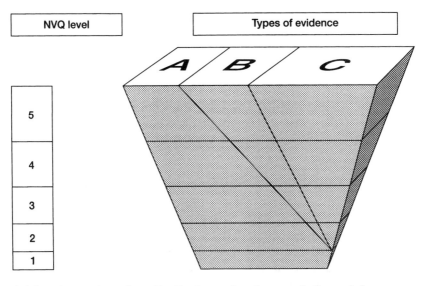

A Inferred competence from directly observed performance in the workplace
B Inferred competence from assessed real-time work-related activities
C Demonstration of underpinning knowledge and understanding and skills through work simulations and tests

Figure 12.1 Hamlin and Stewart's model (2)

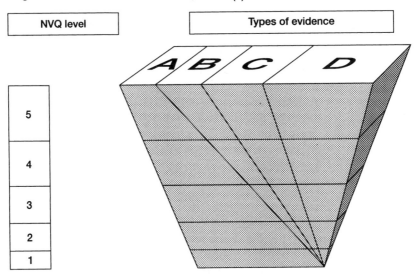

A Inferred competence from directly observed performance in the workplace
B Inferred competence from assessed real-time work-related activities
C Demonstration of underpinning knowledge and understanding and skills through work simulations and tests
D Demonstration of what theories have informed actions/demonstration of conceptual understanding of how such theories have informed actions

Figure 12.2 Modified version of Hamlin and Stewart's model as developed as developed by Walton

she may be considering whether to do a specialized NVQ in training and development using the TDLB standards, or to go for an MCI award building on their managerial experience. It will require quite thorough questioning of the individual to determine with them how they see their career developing, and what their real needs are. Try to avoid being too directive. The final choice must lie with the candidate, and they must feel committed to whatever they decide to embark upon.

Full award or units

One of the advantages of the NVQ system is that candidates don't need to register for a full qualification but can undertake a limited number of units. Superficially this can seem very attractive. What a candidate is undertaking addresses their immediate developmental needs, and the time-scale to completion is seemingly shortened. At a subsequent stage, if the candidate so wishes, the outstanding units can be attempted.

However, at the higher levels, a number of counter-arguments can be presented to candidates who wish to register for a limited number of units. These include:

- Candidates will be encouraged to produce evidence from reports, projects and other activities, which will almost certainly contribute to a range of units.
- At higher levels, a substantial part of the knowledge and understanding is likely to be domain specific, not unit or element specific.
- At higher levels, jobs are less likely to be compartmentalized into discrete 'standards-related' activities. Managers, for example, are likely to be operating across the MCI range.
- In practice, the production of a portfolio for a limited number of units can take almost as long as a portfolio for a full qualification.

One of the anxieties that candidates might express in requesting accreditation against a limited number of units is that there are some areas of the standards which they don't cover in their work role. This is always worth exploring with them. Sometimes they may be mistaken. Sometimes it is relatively easy for the centre to engineer suitable evidence-generating activities.

NVQ-only centres should consider establishing links with local colleges or universities. Apart from the possibility of getting their programmes credit rated, they will more readily be able to indicate to candidates possible progression routes to further qualifications. Where appropriate, links should be fostered with professional bodies, for similar reasons.

University centres

Some universities offer 'hybrid' programmes whereby candidates can simultaneously obtain an NVQ award and a university qualification. Because of low completion rates and also because of candidates feeling overburdened with the weight of assessment, some university centres are offering a choice of either a post-graduate certificate/diploma, or NVQ level 4/5, or both.

The typical process is as follows:

- The intending candidate contacts relevant university programme area and completes an application form.
- The candidate is interviewed to establish what type of programme would most suit his or her needs; the candidate informed of the range of programmes available and the implications of each programme.
- Candidate is offered either a post-graduate certificate/diploma programme, an NVQ level 4/5, or both or neither, based on their prior learning or experience.
- The candidate registers for qualification chosen.

If the candidate chooses to do both a university post-graduate award and an NVQ qualification, then each award requires a separate registration. Typically, the university award is completed more quickly that the NVQ qualification because the assessment is more narrowly defined. Many universities with accredited NVQ centres are, however, establishing clear relationships between the assessment requirements for the university award and those for the NVQ award in a given programme area.

In the case of linked awards, it would be expected that the university assessments would relate to national NVQ standards and contribute to the portfolio of evidence.

Because the time-scales for completing university post-graduate awards are tighter and the range of assessment narrower, many candidates prefer to undertake the university awards first and then complete their NVQ. It is not that university awards are easier, it is that the task of putting together a comprehensive portfolio of evidence across all units and elements can be very time-consuming, and some performance evidence can be difficult to obtain, with special arrangements having to be made (see also the Sunderland University research, below). The registration process is illustrated diagrammatically in Figure 12.3.

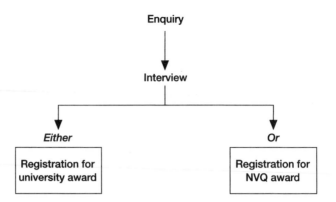

Figure 12.3 The registration process for hybrid programmes

Some universities (and colleges and professional bodies) have two separate organizational structures for NVQ 'syllabus-based' awards. The IPD very clearly differentiates between syllabus-based and NVQ awards. The IPD had to be approved separately by the NCVQ as an awarding body and to have in place an appropriate network of external verifiers and assessors/internal verifiers. Its syllabus-based qualifications are under its own control and do not operate to NVQ national standards.

Pre-competence or capability (potentiality) awards

As discussed in Chapter 6, some centres are experimenting with 'pre-competence' or 'capability' award, designed for candidates who are unemployed. Sunderland University Business School did market research on why large initial interest from prospective candidates for their NVQs using TDLB standards at level 4 did not translate into actual customers. Their findings were that more than half of potential candidates could not undertake NVQs due to the lack of opportunity to demonstrate workplace competence. Reasons included:

- Role incompatibility.
- Self-employment.
- Unemployment.
- Consultants (not in an 'organizational' managerial role).
- Threat of redundancy before they were able to complete their portfolio.
- Fear of a job change before they were able to complete their portfolio.

Sunderland sent an internal report to the NCVQ arguing that, rather than having provided a structure which met the stated aim of increasing access to qualifications, NVQs actually erected barriers compared with the forms of 'prescribed' learning prevalent in traditional higher education driven qualifications.

Sunderland use their post-graduate certificate and diploma awards in human resources development as 'pre-competence' or 'capability' awards. These awards, in addition to giving post-graduate credits, recognize that the candidate has achieved both the underlying knowledge and understanding relating to, and satisfactory simulation of, competent performance corresponding to the NVQ. Sunderland also consider that such capability awards are a predictor of competence.

Non-university centres offering a range of programmes

Such centres range from further education colleges to independent consultancies. The process of giving advice to candidates should not differ substantially from that given by other types of centre. Some centres have developed strong links with universities – indeed, a number of centres are loosely attached to a parent university such as the Accredited Training Centre of the University of West of England. Such links should be of major benefit to candidates because they help clarify progression opportunities.

Example of collaboration between university and non-university partners

Some centres operating outside the university system have been developing pre-competence awards at the higher levels for candidates who, for a variety of reasons, cannot aim for an NVQ. For example, in the TDLB area, an independent consultancy, Development Processes UK Ltd, in conjunction with Thames Valley University, delivers a development programme leading to pre-competence awards for those individuals who cannot demonstrate competence at the workplace. Specific categories of people targeted include:

- Those who are unemployed.
- Those who are employed but lack employer support or who wish to gain qualifications without the knowledge of their employer.
- Those who are employed who wish to gain an human resources development (HRD) qualification prior to moving into an HRD role.
- Those who are employed who have a limited HRD role and cannot meet S/NVQ demands in terms of assessment.

These qualifications are intended to be syllabus-based qualifications to underpin NVQs by incorporating the knowledge and understanding required for an NVQ. A deliberate attempt is made to incorporate assessment methods which will enable candidates to generate evidence for a portfolio which could, if required, be presented for separate or subsequent NVQ assessment. The ethos is very similar to that at the University of Sunderland (see above), but no post-graduate credits are awarded.

Centre guidance for candidates

Irrespective of the type of centre, the following guidelines should be relevant:

- Have a clearly identified contact person to whom intending candidates can speak about the range of possibilities.
- Interview intending candidates. Don't rely on information from application forms.
- Develop a set of predetermined questions to ask candidates. (Some useful questions are provided below.)
- Have a chart on display which shows both horizontal relationships between qualifications and vertical progression routes. Many professional bodies, which have introduced NVQs but have maintained syllabus-based programmes. Try to show how these compare in terms of membership status.
- Provide brochures which clearly indicate these relationships, as well as any entry requirements.
- Have available, if possible, sample portfolios, so that candidates can get a feel of the requirements of an NVQ before they commit themselves.
- Have available biographies of previous candidates, indicating the qualification they attempted, how long it took them to complete, their job role, what went well and what went less well. There is a temptation in publicity material to refer only to successes. Examples of candidates who didn't complete because they enrolled for the wrong programme, for example, or lacked organization support could also be helpful.
- Organize a special 'information day' where intending candidates can meet the programme team, and some previous candidates and their mentors.

Questions to ask intending candidates

- What knowledge do you have of NVQs? What do you consider to be the key features of an NVQ?
- Have you ever been on an NVQ programme?
- What do you understand by the term 'portfolio of evidence'?
- Have you seen the standards? What evidence do you think you can provide already?
- What level of NVQ are you considering?
- Do you have any organizational support?
- What is your current employment status?
- What is your current job role?
- Have you come across the concept of 'mentor'? Do you have a mentor in mind? Have you discussed the position with him or her?
- What academic qualifications do you possess?
- What mode of study are you intending?
- Why are you interested in an NVQ programme? What are the advantages to you of obtaining one in this area?
- Are you interested in professional body membership?
- Have you considered a professional body or post-graduate diploma?
- Would you be prepared to do a preparatory, pre-competence award?

Scenario 1

Colin has come to you asking for advice about a further qualification. He left school at 16 with five O levels at grade C or above, including English but not Maths. For eight years he worked for a building society in a general administrative capacity, until he was made redundant. During his two-year period of redundancy he enrolled on a national pilot and successfully completed an Advanced GNVQ in Management. He has recently returned to full-time employment in a junior management capacity for a city insurance firm. They would sponsor him for a relevant qualification. What would you recommend?

Scenario 2

Folashade is in her early 30s with ten years' managerial experience in a housing association. She has ten members of staff reporting to her and has significant budgetary responsibility. She completed an HNC in Business Studies six years ago. She is undecided as to whether to go for a traditional post-graduate Diploma in Management Studies or whether to aim for an MCI II award. What would you recommend?

Scenario 3

Derek is a relatively senior manager in a manufacturing company which is trying for investors-in-people status. He had intended to do an MBA by distance learning but, like a number of his colleagues, has been instructed that he must have an MCI II qualification in two years' time as part of his continuous personal development within the company. He thinks he can do it all by APL and do his MBA at the same time. What would you recommend?

For suggested answers see Chapter 17.

References

1 Walton J. et al. (1995) *Qualifications Mapping Project – Training and Development S/NVQs and Academic Qualifications,* Employment Department Summer.
2 *Guide to National Vocational Qualifications,* March 1991.
3 Hamlin R. and Stewart J. (1994) *Competence-based Qualifications: Maintaining Forward Momentum (Competence and Assessment),* January.

13 How to handle assessment and accreditation of prior learning

Objectives

By the end of this chapter you should be able to

1 Define accreditation of prior learning (APL) and differentiate between accreditation of prior certificated learning and lccreditation of prior experiential learning.
2 Identify the key features of the role of the APL advisor.
3 Understand the role of the candidate in the APL process.
4 Be clear as to the nature of the support systems required for APL candidates.

Introduction

The S/NVQ assessment model recognizes evidence from prior achievements as an important and legitimate way of demonstrating competence. The role of APL in the S/NVQ assessment model is demonstrated in the 1991 guide to NVQs (1) as shown in Figure 13.1.

Accreditation of prior learning (APL) is the NVQ term used when candidates use evidence from past achievement to gain credit for their competence. The intention is that by giving credit for a candidate's existing competence, APL speeds up the qualification process and enables learning to be carefully targeted to individual needs (1995 *NVQ Criteria and Guidance* (2: pp. 30–31)). Thus APL is basically using historical evidence to demonstrate current competence.

Susan Simosko defines APL as:

... a process that enables people to gain recognition and certification for what they already know and can do, often acquired without the benefit of formal instruction. It encourages people to draw on their own unique experiences, identifying and equating what they have learned to the standards of particular qualifications. It also requires individuals to take an active role in their own assessment and as such reflect on their real strengths and development needs.(3: p. 5)

APL can be given for a whole qualification or for specific units or elements that make up a qualification. The 1991 NVQ Criteria (1) stated that 'NCVQ requires awarding bodies to provide APL, which

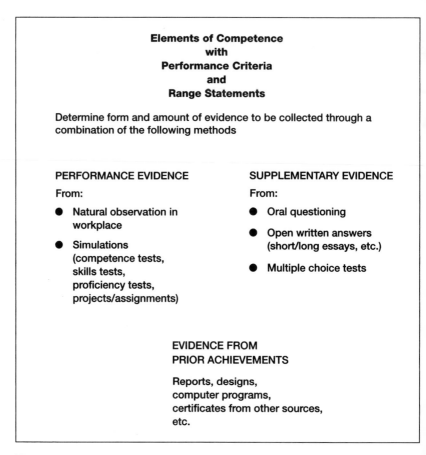

Figure 13.1 The role of the APL in S/NVQ assessment (from *Guide to National Vocational Qualifications*, NCVQ, March 1991, p. 22)

particularly benefits adult learners and those without formal training'. In some quarters this was interpreted that a discrete APL route had to be offered to candidates by all centres seeking NVQ accreditation. The 1995 criteria (2) modified the requirement as follows:

Awarding bodies should ensure that centres take full account of all candidates' evidence of prior achievement. (2: p. 30)

In practice, most candidates will require some form of topping-up process, either for parts of units or for whole units.

Some NVQ candidates might feel that they can demonstrate competence in all the standards associated with a particular qualification without doing any additional work. They are in for a rude awakening. APL is not a simple process of individuals coming into an NVQ centre with a number of reports they have written and supporting letters of attestation to how good they are in their job, and asking how many units they can be credited with. Assessment by APL is not an easy option. The standards to be demonstrated are exactly the same as a candidate going through a conventional tuition process. Evidence has to be contextualized against the standards they are aimimg for and presented in a way which is meaningful to the assessor. APL is very much a candidate-led process, with the onus on individuals to justify their claims. Normally, individuals would need to do this through the medium of a portfolio – in the same way as other NVQ candidates.

Candidates can submit a portfolio for APL consisting almost entirely of product evidence – documents/reports produced at some time in the past. However, there may well be some requirement in particular elements/units for observation of an activity to be conducted by an approved assessor, and this may have to be independently demonstrated outside of the APL process.

Often it is remarkably difficult to find sufficient suitable evidence to verify what one has done in the past and thus justify claims to competence. I have frequently been confronted with people who have said 'I did that in my last job, but threw all the records away when I left'. A general piece of advice to all intending NVQ applicants for higher level awards, never mind those seeking APL is: *'Throw nothing away'*!

It can also be a very lonely business putting together evidence for assessment purposes outside of the support structure of a programme of study.

Some NVQ candidates considering APL might hope that they can gain a particular qualification without undertaking any formal learning. This is increasingly less likely at the higher levels, given the recent introduction of knowledge-and-understanding specifications into the standards. Candidates will need to demonstrate that they have access to a body of knowledge sufficiently broad and comprehensive to satisfy these supplementary evidence requirements.

APL is often subdivided into:

- *Accreditation of prior certificated learning*, where credit can be given to qualifications already attained.
- *Accreditation of prior experiential learning*, where credit can be given for activities and products of activities previously undertaken which have never been recognized for qualification purposes.

Accreditation of prior certificated learning (APCL)

There are two possible ways of accrediting prior certificated learning.

- A whole qualification which is undertaken outside of the NVQ system is recognized as having equivalent status to an NVQ award. This is an unlikely occurrence.

- Assessments that a candidate has undertaken in a non-NVQ qualification are treated as providing sufficient evidence to lead to unit or element accreditation.

It is difficult, unless the qualification is formatted in a way which demonstrates linkages to NVQs, to provide APL credits for qualifications which are not linked to the NVQ system, without a lot of interpretive work being done by the candidate. Thus, for a qualification which had not been designed with NVQ considerations in mind, it could be possible for an assessor to give some element/unit accreditation, but only if enormous amounts of time were spent on establishing the linkages. This would entail sitting down (with, say, a management report) and cross-mapping it with the standards.

In reality, this is not feasible as the process would be too time-consuming and not a cost-effective use of the assessor's time. At higher levels it would have to be a candidate-driven process, in which candidates take responsibility for cross-mapping the assessments taken for a previous qualification against the NVQ/units claimed. This requires of the candidate considerable understanding, both of the standards and of the resulting assessment process.

Clearly, it would help if the designers of non-NVQ qualifications were to give some thought to the NVQ standards for the associated occupational areas which are likely to be assessed subsequently in some form or other. This could be demonstrated by a form of words similar to the following: *'Assignment A – on completion of this assignment you should have produced evidence against MCI I (say) elements X, Y and Z'.* This can provide helpful guidance for both candidates and subsequent S/NVQ assessors.

Accreditation of prior experiential learning (APEL)

It is not clear from the published guidelines how far back in time one can go for accreditable evidence. The February 1994 guide *Implementing the National Standards for Assessment and Verification* (4) states that evidence of prior achievement/experience should be accepted wherever it is clearly relevant to the national standard, is authenticated, and the candidate's competence can be confirmed as current. But no time-scale is provided for currency. I have heard various figures given – from three years back to five years back, but have never seen these in print. Most assessors would be reluctant to go back further than five years for a given piece of evidence, but each individual case should be treated on its merits.

Gealy et al. (5) argue that competence can deteriorate over time. Skill decay may mean that the candidate can no longer perform to the required standard. A long time gap may also mean that the whole knowledge base has changed, which would include principles as well as methods and facts. A good example of such rapid change is in the sphere of information technology. The authors go on to say that there are no hard-and-fast rules that can be applied to decide when evidence is no longer current. Assessors will have to decide what is the typical speed of loss of competence and what is a reasonable time for relearning before accepting prior experience as evidence.

It is important to recognize the equal-opportunities implications. It is a requirement that NVQs are free from overt or covert discriminatory practices with regard to gender, age, race or creed and are designed to pay due regard to the special needs of the individuals. Being too restrictive about the idea of currency can curtail opportunities for groups such as those who have undertaken parenting/family responsibilities, been out of the employment market for a period of time, and yet in a previous role have met fully the national standards in a given occupational area.

As an approach to gaining a qualification, APL is not restricted to the NVQ system. A number of universities allow students to gain an award without going through a formal course of study, but by completing a range of predetermined assignments

In 1988 the Council for National Academic Awards (CNAA) produced a briefing document entitled *Assessment of Prior Experiential Learning* (6) to advise university (then polytechnic) centres how to address the issue for their awards. The recommendations included:

- Provision of opportunities for students to discuss and reflect on their relevant professional experience, focus on their learning outcomes and develop ways of documenting this for presentation for accreditation.
- Provision of individual counselling sessions to facilitate identification and assessment of prior learning.

The onus is on persons seeking credit to demonstrate the level of the activity and its relevance to their professional development.

Typical approach by a university to APEL

Where APEL provision is offered by universities as a route to accreditation for awards, the university assessor typically evaluates the following to determine the extent of credit that can be afforded for the activities that students have undertaken:

- The professional benefits that the students can demonstrate they have obtained through participation in the activities.

> - The extent to which these benefits can be demonstrated to be at master's level, i.e. demonstration of higher level cognitive skills.
> - The role of the student in the activity.
> - The time and effort devoted to the activity.
> - The extent to which the activity was an appropriate means of obtaining the benefits.
> - The opportunities students have had for reflection on and analysis of the activity. What have they used to assist them in their reflections? Examples might include:
>   (a) reading undertaken,
>   (b) writing undertaken, and
>   (c) discussion with others.
>
> The assessment process should include corroboration of the applicant's assertions.

This APEL process is very similar to that for NVQ awards, but there are some marked differences to past NVQ practice:

- The emphasis on reflection
- The need to demonstrate higher order cognitive skills

It could well be that at higher levels there will be increasing evidence of NVQ candidates demonstrating these skills in their portfolios. Should this prove to be the case this will afford greater congruence than in the past between the traditional academic and the NVQ systems.

The APL adviser's role

The importance afforded to APL in the NVQ system is demonstrated by the existence of a discrete Training and Development Lead Body (TDLB) unit covering the APL advisory function. D36 Advise and Support Candidates to Identify Prior Achievement covers what is often called the 'APL advisor's role'. It consists of three elements:

- D361 Help the candidate to identify relevant achievements.
- D362 Agree and review an action plan for achieving qualifications.
- D363 Help the candidate to prepare and present evidence for assessment.

The August 1994 guidance notes, *The National Standards for Assessment and Verification* (7), state that the unit applies to any advisor who helps candidates to identify prior achievements relevant to the target qualifications and to present evidence of assessment. However, it does not cover the assessment itself, which is specified in D33.

The notes go on to say that the advisory element in the role is of particular importance in helping a candidate make realistic decisions about both the award to aim for and the nature of evidence to target. The advisor must demonstrate knowledge of the national system of assessment and certification as well as the qualifications a candidate is striving for. The three elements of D36 cover distinct aspects of the advisory function, although in practice it is quite difficult to separate them out. There are also few advisors who are not also assessors.

D361　*Help the candidate to identify relevant achievements*

The performance criteria for this element are quite clear and helpful. They cover:

- Giving the candidates clear and accurate information about the reasons for, and methods of, collecting evidence of prior achievement.
- Encouraging candidates to review all relevant experience.
- Accurately identifying national standards from the review of experience which a candidate may potentially be able to achieve currently.
- Encouraging self-confidence and self-esteem in candidates by support, and the way it is given.
- Explaining options open to candidates in a clear and constructive way, especially if they express disagreement with the advice offered.

Some candidates will come to an NVQ assessment centre with the specific purpose of getting prior achievement recognized. There will also be students on non-NVQ programmes who may wish to know whether their qualification will contribute towards an NVQ award. Additionally, candidates attending a programme of study with an NVQ focus, such as the Institute of Management (IM) Certificate in Management will wish to know what standards they are aiming for and what prior achievement they may be able to draw upon in portfolio of evidence. Many colleges and universities spend a substantial period of time at the beginning of such programme of study explaining how prior achievement may be incorporated into a portfolio. This introduction invariably needs to be reviewed at regular intervals as candidates become more familiar with the standards and the types of product and process evidence they can draw upon.

D362 Agree and review an action plan for achieving qualifications

Although this is a separate element of D36, in practice it is quite difficult to separate out from D361. It is highly likely that an action plan will emerge as a result of the advice given. This is demonstrated by the overlap of the performance criteria.

For example, compare the D362 performance criterion (a)

. . . candidates are given accurate advice and appropriate encouragement to enable them to form realistic expectations of the value and relevance of prior achievements . . .

with the D361 performance criterion (a)

. . . the candidate is given clear and accurate information about the reasons for and methods of collelcting and presenting evidence of prior achievements.

Also, compare D362 performance criterion (b)

. . . target vocational qualifications identified are appropriate to candidate's prior achievements and future aspirations

with D361 performance criterion (c)

. . . national standards which the candidate may potentially be able to achieve currently are accurately identified from the review of experience

D363 Help the candidate to collect and present evidence for assessment

The performance criteria for this element emphasize the support needed to be given to candidates to help them put together a portfolio of evidence. This issue is addressed in detail in Chapter 13.

One of the performance criteria focuses on identifying opportunities for candidates to demonstrate achievement where evidence from prior experience is not available. In practice, this criterion overlaps with the other two elements of D36 and would probably be addressed in an induction programme.

Simosko (3) suggests that there is a six-stage process associated with the provision of an APL service:

Stage 1: Pre-entry

Candidates receive information about APL, attend either a group briefing session or meet individually with an APL advisor, and decide whether or not to proceed with APL.

Many potential candidates will have very little idea what is involved in claimimg APL. A preliminary counselling interview with the candidate should ascertain whether a candidate has sufficient relevant experience and is likely to be able to produce adequate supporting evidence to satisfy the assessment criteria.

Stage 2: Candidate profiling

Candidates:

- Reflect on their own experiences and accomplishments.
- Compare themselves against national standards or learning outcomes using checklists or other written materials.
- Develop a profile of themselves against these standards or learning outcomes.
- Identify useful sources and types of evidence.
- Identify areas needing top-up training.

Stage 3: Gathering of evidence

Candidates:

- Gather and/or produce physical evidence for each of the elements of competence or learning outcomes in the qualifications they are seeking.
- Produce portfolios of evidence in a structured manner.
- Receive guidance and support through individual APL advisors and/or peer support groups.
- Use written materials throughout to guide their portfolio-preparation work.

Stage 4: Assessment

Candidates:

- Are assessed by trained subject specialists in each of the areas in which they are seeking recognition.
- Produce additional evidence, most often during an oral interview with their assessors.

Stage 5: Accreditation

Candidates:

- Receive some or all of the credit they were originally seeking.

Stage 6: Post-assessment guidance

Candidates:

- Review the outcomes of their assessment with a trained advisor.

Example

This APL model was developed as a result of a number of projects funded by the Employment Department between 1989 and 1991. One of these was an Management Charter Initiative (MCI) project for experienced managers, with three different awarding bodies participating. Conclusions from this project included:

- APL proved to be a technique for development, not just a retrospective of past accomplishments.
- Focusing on current accomplishments enabled managers to make better use of the standards.
- The development of a portfolio seemed beneficial to those with considerable as well as those with minimal experience.
- Managers benefitted most from working in groups and having prescriptive guidance about the development of their portfolios.
- Evidence from non-paid work was entirely acceptable provided that it met the standards.

The MCI project indicated that, at higher levels, where candidates are unlikely to have significant literacy problems and are relatively clear about the areas in which they want/need accreditation, they can proceed on their own with much of the APL process. However, they do need the back-up of clear and accurate written guidance. Based on the MCI project it is suggested that centres/awarding bodies provide APL workbooks which:

- Brief candidates about APL and the benefits that could accrue from completing the process.
- Offer background information about the specific occupational standards aimed for.
- Provide the standards in checklist form so that candidates can, in their own time, reflect on them and compare their own experiences and accomplishments.
- Offer guidance on the development of a career profile so that candidates can systematically link their own competences to those described in the standards.
- Provide all the necessary forms candidates need to complete.
- Describe the nature of acceptable evidence.
- Clarify the roles of advisors and assessors.
- Provide information to help candidates prepare for their assessments, in particular their assessment interviews.

The more prescriptive centres can be about the presentation of the final portfolio, the easier it is for the candidates to compile and for the assessors to review and assess. Even for more conventional development programmes it is helpful to recommend a standard portfolio format. Where candidates are conducting such a significant part of the process on their own, then such prescription is even more important.

APL is not an easy route to obtaining an award, and a number of candidates drop by the wayside. Without quantifying them Simosko (3) gave the following common reasons for dropping out:

- Lack of time.
- Other commitments.
- Difficulty getting to centre.
- Difficulty obtaining evidence.
- Too expensive.
- More work than anticipated.
- Health problems.
- Other delivery methods were more appropriate.

Those who did complete were, on the whole, complementary about the APL process, reporting it as 'satisfying', 'challenging', 'rewarding', 'helpful', etc.

Question 4

Should candidates for APL be offered an induction programme? What form might it take? Would follow-up sessions be required?

For a suggested answer, see Chapter 17.

References

1 NVQ Criteria and Guidance, NCVQ, March 1991.
2 NVQ Criteria and Guidance, NCVQ, January 1995.
3 Simosko S. (1992) *Embedding Accreditation of Prior Learning* (Competence and Assessment Briefing Series No. 7), October.
4 *Implementing the National Standards for Assessment and Verification*, NCVQ, February 1994.
5 Gealy N., Johnson C., Miller C. and Mitchell L. (1991) in: *Development of Assessable Standards for National Certification*, (ed. Fennell E.), Employment Department.
6 *Assessment of Prior Experiential Learning*, CNAA, 1988.
7 *The National Standards for Assessment and Verification*, TDLB, August 1994.

14 How to help candidates put a portfolio of evidence together

Objectives

By the end of this chapter you should be able to:

1 Define the term 'portfolio' as used in an NVQ context.
2 Differentiate between candidate-led and assessor-led portfolios.
3 Describe the basic structure and components of a portfolio.
4 Identify the types of evidence that candidates should present in thei portfolios.
5 Indicate ways in which evidence of knowledge, understanding anc critical reflection can be presented.
6 Establish the role of the Awarding Body, the assessment centre and the NVQ assessors and advisors in the process.

Introduction

Debling and Stuart (1) emphasize the role of the candidate, especially at the higher levels, in packaging evidence and putting it in a form acceptable for assessors. Given the significance of the candidate's role in collecting evidence from a variety of sources for assessment, it i very important to give appropriate advice to candidates on how they should present this evidence. It is also helpful to assessors and verifier if candidates for a given award adopt a similar approach in indexing and formatting their information. Many awarding bodies recommenc that candidates adopt a portfolio approach to collecting and present ing evidence, and have provided further guidance as to how such portfolio should be constructed.

The idea of a portfolio of visual evidence is by no means new and ha been used extensively by some professions for many years. Typically designers and architects are accustomed to being asked to provid examples of their work in support of proposals and tenders. Quit often such professionals may be obliged to submit their personal port folios to an employer when seeking a new appointment or promotion The most common form of supporting evidence in such a situation would probably include examples drawn from successful project such as photographs, plans and drawings. This might be supplemented by testimonials, project reports and other specific outputs of thei work.

For a manager seeking to carry out a similar portfolio-based approach to collecting and presenting material, the evidence drawn upon needs to be broad enough to reflect the competence demands of his or her particular job. The portfolio should provide a record of learning and development achievements over a specified period of time. The individual can then use it as a basis for self-reflection and review and others can see and comment on it as appropriate.

According to the Institute of Management (IM), the portfolio provides candidates, their mentors, future employers, tutors and others in a position to assist in the learning process, with a continuous record of analysis of need, development and competence achieved. The thinking of the awarding bodies is influenced by the importance attached in the *National Standards for Assessment and Verification* (2) to helping candidates put together a portfolio of evidence. This is particularly addressed in Element D363 of the Training and Development Lead Body (TDLB) Unit D36, which is concerned with advising and supporting candidates to identify prior achievement (Figure 14.1).

Surprisingly enough, outside of this particular element there is no further reference to a portfolio in the *National Standards for Assessment and Verification*. However, their use in practice extends far beyond a retrospective search for historical evidence which is implied by the term 'prior achievement'. This broader perspective is reflected in the mention of portfolios in the January 1995 *NVQ Criteria and Guidance*:

Evidence is often collated and presented in portfolios. Collating evidence in a portfolio is often taken to be a candidate-led process of collecting and structuring evidence. This can reduce the assessor's workload, and promote candidate involvement and responsibility for their own assessment where appropriate. (3: p. 31)

The guide states that overreliance on paper-based methods of presenting information, such as a portfolio, is seen as a barrier by some candidates, and argues that awarding bodies should provide guidance to centres so that alternatives to portfolios are available in order to ensure that there is access to fair assessment for all candidates. However, at the higher levels it is difficult to see what would constitute a realistic alternative to the portfolio. For managers' jobs, in particular, it would seem to be a most appropriate form of approach, especially given standards such as Record and Store Information (Element 9.3 of Management II Unit 9 Seek, Evaluate and Organize Information for Action).

The February 1994 guidelines for *Implementing the National Standards for Assessment and Verification* (4) give a more developed analysis. They state that, in the broadest sense of the term, a portfolio of evidence for an S/NVQ, or units thereof: '. . . is the whole of the evidence being presented to support a candidate's claim to competence'. This is how a

---

Unit

D36 Advise and Support Candidates to Identify Prior Achievement

Element

D363 Help the candidate to collect and present evidence for assessment

Performance Criteria

a The candidate is provided with suitable support to prepare a portfolio of evidence

b Guidance provided to the candidate during portfolio preparation encourages the efficient development of clear, structured evidence relevant to the units being claimed

c Liaison with assessors establishes mutually convenient arrangements for review of portfolio and maintains the candidate's confidence

d Opportunities are identified for the candidate to demonstrate achievement where evidence from prior experience is not available

e Awarding body documentation, recording and procedural requirements are met

f If there is disagreement with the advice given, options available to the candidate are explained clearly and constructively

Range Statements

1 Support
One to one; group; self study

2 Portfolio content
Evidence from naturally occurring opportunities: evidence from other opportunit
Performance evidence: knowledge evidence

3 Candidates
Young and mature adults; employed, unemployed
With special assessment requirements
With differing levels of confidence

Figure 14.1   Element D363 of TDLB Unit D36

portfolio is commonly understood. Thus the 1995 Institute of Personnel and Development (IPD) *Personal Development and Assessment Guide* (5) defines a portfolio as 'a collection of evidence and information which demonstrates a person's ability and achievements'.

The 1994 guidelines (4) adopt the term 'portfolio approach' to indicate a candidate-led process of collecting and structuring evidence, which can assist in both:

- Reducing the assessor's workload.
- Promoting candidate involvement and responsibility for their own assessment.

The guidelines emphasize that competence, not presentation, must be assessed, and suggest that a candidate-led portfolio approach of this kind can be particularly appropriate in collecting a variety of forms of evidence where direct observation of candidates' performance by an assessor is not easily accessible. The portfolio approach, they contend, should increase access to assessment, not cause unnecessary barriers, and other approaches to evidence collection outside 'candidate-led' portfolios can be equally valid:

> For example, observation of performance by an assessor, supplemented by 1–1 questioning, may be an equally valid way of collecting evidence of competence. The assessors' records of these observations and of the candidate's answers to questions would form an equally valid portfolio. (4: p. 4)

The guidelines go on to make the point that this type of assessor-led approach has cost implications in terms of assessor time, and may lead to only minimal candidate involvement. Nevertheless, 'it does have the advantage of not imposing additional demands on candidates for whom taking responsibility for collecting and structuring their evidence is a barrier to fair assessment'. (4: p. 4)

At the higher levels it can be expected that, although there will be evidence in a given portfolio of assessor-led approaches in respect of, say, records made of work visits, the onus of putting the portfolio together will lie with the individual candidate.

The guidelines distinguish between portfolios used for developmental purposes and those used for national S/NVQ certification. For developmental purposes, portfolios may include action plans, development plans, formative assessments, etc., which are not required for qualification purposes.

It is also suggested that candidates regularly review the evidence they are collecting for their portfolios with a view to selecting only those pieces which most effectively and efficiently prove their competence. This should include, wherever possible, evidence which can contribute to several elements simultaneously. This recommendation is made:

- To speed up the evidence-collection process.
- To reduce the spread and volume of evidence presented.
- To encourage candidates to think in a more holistic way about the standards and how individual elements and units relate to each other.

It should not be thought that a candidate is working on their evidence collection in isolation. It should be the responsibility of a given

centre to provide support mechanisms as detailed in D36 referred t
above.

The 'filing-cabinet' approach to portfolio construction

There has been a lot of criticism of the 'filing-cabinet' approach t
portfolio building. This is epitomized by volumes of evidence fror
various memos, work-placed documents, etc., being presented b
candidates without any thought seemingly being given to explainin
the meaning or relevance of evidence. The sheer weight of documer
tation is expected to so impress the assessors that credit is bound to b
given.

This sort of approach gives no evidence of a candidate having gor
round the Kolb experiential learning cycle of experience – reflection
conceptualization – experimentation. There is not even any indicatio
that a candidate has gone round the mini cycle of experience – refle
tion – experience. There is, in fact, no evidence as such of learnin
having taken place at all. Documents which are cross-reference
against a standard of competence with no covering explanation give n
evidence even of reflection having taken place.

Ways of contextualizing evidence

MCI personal report

The Management Charter Initiative (MCI) 1990 Assessment guidelin
(6) suggest that evidence of performance at work can take the form of
personal report – a description of the actions that have or would hav
to be undertaken. The personal report may be a narrative statemer
produced in written form or it may be oral evidence given in an inte
view where the manager responds to the questions of the assessor. Th
potential content of the report can usefully reflect the stages of th
experiential learning cycle, but the actual content and emphasis
any individual report should be geared to the standards.

The actual content of the personal report should include:

* Details of the actions taken.
* Reflections on actions taken – this can include questions on what a
  manager would have done if the situation had been slightly different
  and thus addresses issues of contingency and understanding.
* Knowledge of what was done and why.

Story-boards

Some awarding bodies require that candidates provide a story-board or narrative account to contextualize each piece of evidence. The 1992 IPD guidelines state that a storyboard is an ideal opportunity for a candidate to describe the sequence and rationale of performance in respect of a piece of evidence and to demonstrate knowledge and understanding of the principles and theory applied relevant to the element. The storyboard differs from the MCI personal report in that the personal report is a description of what took place in lieu of product evidence, whereas a storyboard is an explanation of product evidence such as minutes of meetings, reports, etc., which the candidate has provided.

Note that the IPD use of storyboards refers to contextualizing evidence that has been provided relevant to a given element. Increasingly, there are recommendations coming from the literature and from the field that a given piece of evidence could cover a number of elements and, indeed, units. The January 1995 *NVQ Criteria and Guidance* has this to say:

While evidence requirements are provided on an element by element basis, an assessment guide to the qualification can be useful in taking a qualification-wide view of evidence requirements. It can identify opportunities to collect both performance and knowledge evidence relevant to several elements at once. (3: p. 27)

However, there is no indication from the field that such a 'reflective practitioner' approach to contextualizing evidence is actually taking place in a consistent way.

Case study

On 28 November 1994, a portfolio workshop was held at Nottingham Trent University. The task was to assess seven portfolios, which had all been assessed as adequate for NVQ level 4 TDLB awards, in order to determine whether they could be afforded any post-graduate credit rating.

The assessors were all accredited assessors for TDLB level 4 qualifications and possessed the appropriate D Units. Two were also external verifiers, and one of these was the chief external verifier of the Institute of Personnel and Development (IPD) and not a member of an academic institution. Additionally, the assessors were accustomed to working within the university system and were running programmes or assessing programmes which led to post-graduate awards.

The portfolios had been obtained from a range of assessment centres (two from City and Guilds, three from the IPD, one from the Royal Society for the Encouragement of Arts, Manufacturers and Commerce (RSA) and one from a university programme). Each portfolio was scrutinized independently by at least two assessors. Each assessor then reported back their views on the portfolios, and their comments were recorded on flip-chart sheets. The analysis revealed the following.

Portfolio 1

Barely of S/NVQ quality. Structured around range indicators, not cross-referenced, it was purely descriptive and without any discussion of theory or underpinning knowledge. There was no reflection on practice or on concepts. Judged by one assessor a 'worst case scenario for S/NVQs', it included unsubstantiated and suspect assertions such as: 'the information is valid and reliable as it is provided by the learners immediately following the delivery of training'.

Portfolio 2

Evidence judged to be inadequate to meet S/NVQ competence. The range indicators were not covered. No evidence of underpinning knowledge and understanding within an essentially passive approach. No discussion of why things were done.

Portfolio 4

On the evidence available this was judged inadequate for S/NVQ level 4. There was no storyboard, no rationale and no reasoning.

Portfolios 5 and 6

There was evidence of positive and helpful support and coaching. The storyboard gave good accounts of what had been done. Nevertheless, there was an absence of theoretical models to indicate what had informed the judgments made. For example, there was a copy of a test given at the start of interviewing, but no evaluation based on theories of testing. The overall approach was comprehensive but atomistic. There was little evidence of ownership or use of 'I'. With little discussion of theory, there were no evaluations of options or professional judgments. The two portfolios were descriptive rather than evaluative.

Portfolio 7

This was the only portfolio which came from the university sector and had been constructed to enable the candidate to achieve a dual accreditation, i.e. an NVQ award and a post-graduate certificate. The portfolio was seen to be systematically constructed, with good evidence of effective analysis and reflection, both in the personal reports and in the assignment reports. Although gathered from discrete experiences, evidence was presented holistically. There was excellent evidence of theoretical underpinning and candidate support.

The conclusions of the workshop were that the sample portfolios did not, on the whole, generally follow the guidelines purported to be followed by assessors and centres of assessment, while recognizing that the small sample size was too limited to support any criticisms of the quality-assurance process of awarding bodies.

Example

Sunderland University Business School has developed a helpful approach to addressing contextualizing evidence in Part B of the portfolio guidelines they give out to candidates. Sunderland University provides the following guidance for portfolio building:

As a candidate on an NVQ programme you are required to submit a portfolio for each unit of the NVQ. The portfolio should be presented in the following way.

Title page

Identifying   Candidate name
Contact address/telephone number
Programme candidate registered on
Unit title and reference

Personal profile

This gives background information on the candidate for the benefit of any assessor who does not know him/her. The profile should include

A CV
A description of current job role

Personal report

This is in two parts

Part A

Part A of the candidate report should give a description of any essential background information to the performance evidence provided in the portfolio. It should 'set the scene' for the assessor – enabling him/her to gain an understanding of the context of actions undertaken. It should also include a narrative account of actions and significant events. This account must be cross-referenced to:

- Elements, performance criteria and range indicators of the Unit.
- Any performance evidence contained in the portfolio.

A simple way to do this is to use the Element Titles and Perform-ance Criteria as headings to structure the report.

Part B

In Part B of the personal report candidates should describe:

- why they performed the tasks identified in the Unit in the way they did
- what alternative ways they considered
- what theory/conceptual knowledge they used in guiding their actions
- what they felt they learned from their experiences
- what they or their organization could do to improve performance in this area of the Standards.

Part B is an opportunity to show understanding of relevant theory and of the thinking process behind actions.

Some other university centres have adopted an alternative approach to Part B. They ask that candidates produce integrative pre-set assign-ments or 'special projects'. An example might be to produce a market-ing plan. Such assignments are designed to produce knowledge and understanding evidence across a range of units – what is sometimes called 'domain-specific knowledge' as opposed to 'element/unit specific' knowledge. Candidates are given an indication of the per-formance evidence elements and associated performance criteria that might be addressed by the assignment, but it is up to each candidate to provide sufficient supporting evidence of competence.

Portfolio guidelines from awarding bodies

In essence a portfolio should take the form of a folder, file or similar, within which is presented

- A personal profile of the candidate.
- Evidence of competence and development.

The IPD Awarding Body recommends that a binder is used to contain the evidence collected. The binder should be clearly marked 'Portfolio'. There should be a title page or front cover to identify:

- The title of the qualification or unit.
- Candidate's name.
- The name of the awarding body.
- The name of the candidate's organization, if relevant.
- The volume number if the portfolio is likely to run to more than one volume.

The BTEC/Council for National Academic Awards (CNAA) 1990 Guidelines on *The Assessment of Management Competences* (7) emphasize that however the evidence is presented:

. . .candidates will own their own records of competence and, in submitting themselves for assessment, should be encouraged to carry a great deal of the responsibility for arranging, presenting and recording their own assessments. (7: p. 27)

IPD criteria for a 'good' portfolio

The IPD guidelines suggest that if candidates can answer 'yes' to the following questions then the ingredients of a good portfolio are probably present:

- Can assessors find their way around the portfolio easily?
- Is there no irrelevant padding?
- Is it easy to read?
- Is there a system referencing evidence to elements and performance criteria?
- Is the sequence of presentation logical and helpful?
- Can all of the contents be understood?
- Is the evidence clearly valid, authentic, current and sufficient?
- Does it show the candidate's contribution to achieving the organization's objectives and help continuously to improve its performance?

Presentation of portfolios

Many awarding bodies provide packs giving guidance on how to construct portfolios, i.e. Candidate Process Packs or Professional Development Portfolio packs. Examples include the Institute of Marketing (IM) and IPD guidelines.

M guidelines

As a general framework, the following headings are suggested for inclusion in the portfolio:

- A detailed CV.
- A detailed job description of the candidate's current and most recent post.
- The function of the organization and the work of the candidate's present department.
- The organization, structure and departmental layout.
- Definition of the work undertaken in the department in (a) managerial terms and (b) the technical scenario of the process, defining outputs, customers, etc.
- Experience gained, i.e. what has been done and what is planned for the future.
- If possible, a copy of the last appraisal and progress made, problems experienced and solutions implemented.
- A constructive appraisal of the organization, function and department.
- A constructive appraisal of own training and development.

PD guidelines

The following areas are recommended for inclusion in the portfolio:

- Personal pen picture and a copy of current CV.
- Any relevant qualifications, with copies of certificates awarded.
- Organization profile.
- Glossary of terms.
- List of people who have been helping with NVQ development.
- Evidence matrix.
- Evidence.
- Candidate development plans.
- Candidate claim form.
- Assessor report forms.
- Internal verifier report.

Evidence statements or matrices

Some of the guidelines have in the past suggested that there should be element-by-element evidence statements or matrices, each one clearly contextualized against the performance criteria for that element.

Institute of Personnel and Development
Evidence Matrix

ELEMENT NO: ....

ELEMENT TITLE: ....

Ref	Evidence Name / Performance Criteria															Range

The IPD guidelines refer to the production of evidence statements, each one relating to a discrete element of the standards. It is contended that such evidence statements will enable candidates to consider their evidence, element by element, and enable them to examine and summarize their evidence against each of the performance criteria (Figure 14.2).

In my opinion, producing evidence statements is too atomistic if done element by element. One piece of evidence can be contextualized in some circumstances against a range of standards, especially if it is a substantive report, or a set of documents covering a range of activities from problem identification to solution. The element-by-element approach leads to the risk that the resultant portfolios become too mechanistic and narrow in terms of the evidence presented. It also leads to the risk of substantial repetition if the same piece of evidence is used for a number of elements and units.

The IPD guidelines go on to state that as candidates collect and present evidence this will become the biggest part of the portfolio. They also suggest that there should be a subsection for each unit of competence. However, in my opinion there is a risk that if one tackles portfolios on an element-by-element and unit-by-unit basis, there can be considerable repetition. I favour the matrix shown in Figure 14.3 for evidence collection.

Evidence source	Units covered, element by element											
	1.1	1.2	1.3	1.4	1.5	2.1	2.2	2.3	2.4	3.1	3.2	etc.
Report on IT	✗	✗			✗		✗		PC a		PC a/c/d	
Personal report 1	✗	✗	✗	✗	✗							
Personal report 2						✗	✗	✗	✗			
Witness testimony	✗	✗	✗	✗	✗							
etc.												

✗ All the performance criteria have been covered.
PCa, PCa/c/d The piece of evidence covers only
performance criteria a, a/c/d for the element.

Figure 14.3 MCI II evidence matrix

Evidence requirements of portfolios

Portfolios should, in evidence terms, provide information on the following:

Performance

- Performance at the workplace.
- Justifications of why actions undertaken were done in a particular way.
- Descriptions of performance evidence and explanations of candidate's role.

Knowledge and understanding

- Reference to principles and theories drawn upon in specific instances.
- Knowledge of principles and theories that might be drawn upon as part of the 'practitioners' toolkit', but not specifically addressed in the performance evidence.

Cognitive skills

- Demonstration of relationships within what has been learned.
- Evidence that the field of study is seen in an overall perspective.
- Demonstration of some originality in reflection.
- Evidence of judging and comparing actions and products against models of good practice.
- Evidence of problem-seeking and -solving.

At the time of writing, the National Council for Vocational Qualifications (NCVQ) guidelines emphasize that knowledge and understanding must be contextualized against a given standard. However, there is pressure from a number of professional bodies to incorporate 'domain-specific' knowledge. For example, someone demonstrating competence in law would need a general knowledge and understanding of 'contracts', although it is unlikely that this would be contextualized against a particular unit or element.

The Sunderland University Business School model requests that evidence be provided on a unit-by-unit basis. However this could lead to some repetition. It could well be – especially at NVQ levels 4 and 5 – that one integrated activity at the workplace could provide performance evidence against a whole range of elements, and even units. For example, in the management field a candidate might be able to describe their actions in setting up and implementing a specific project, such as introducing quality-improvement teams. Their actions could provide evidence against Management Charter Initiative (MCI) Units such as

- Unit II.1   Initiate and Implement Change and Improvement in Services, Products and Systems.
- Unit II.2   Monitor, Maintain and Improve Service and Product Delivery.
- Unit II.4   Secure Effective Resource Allocation for Activities and Projects.
- Unit II.7   Plan, Allocate and Evaluate Work Carried out by Teams, Individuals and Self.

Types of evidence

Candidates are usually encouraged by assessors and centre guidance notes to incorporate a range of evidence. It is the evidence which will provide the basis for the portfolio. There are three main sources of evidence.

Performance evidence

This can include the following:

Natural observation by an assessor

This would normally take the form of notes by the assessor that a given activity had been observed, the circumstances in which it was carried out, and the extent to which competence was demonstrated. Observation is not only of an activity. It can also include evaluating workplace settings which a candidate has responsibility for. It is important that the assessor's notes and comments are included in the portfolio.

Product evidence from the workplace or other sources

This would include reports, memos, plans, budgets, and so on. Some of these would be the result of current activities carried out during the course of putting the portfolio together. Some would result from previously conducted activities. It is important to ensure that such materials are clearly dated.

Examples of activities conducted at the workplace

There are some activities which can be video recorded or taped. They include tapes/videos of meetings and interviews. These are legitimate ways of generating evidence, although there is some research which suggests that assessors do not listen to tapes or watch the videos as diligently as they might.

Generated evidence

This covers quite a broad sweep. It incorporates any special projects done at work for the purposes of getting together evidence for assessment. It would also include simulations such as interviewing role plays where it is difficult for a candidate to demonstrate suitable direct evidence from the workplace.

Supplementary evidence

The witness testimony

One type of evidence that is often referred to is the witness testimony. This can take two forms:

- A general testimonial taking the form of a reference, and stating that X is a good, competent employee. This is of limited value.
- A statement of authentication by a manager that X has done the work in question. It is usually recommended that this should be on organization letterhead. It can be useful if sparingly done. However, it becomes somewhat repetitive and inappropriate for every piece of evidence to be authenticated independently.

Completed written tests or examinations

Tests and examinations are not precluded under NVQ rules, although they are not commonly drawn upon at the higher levels. Any test or examination would have to be clearly contextualized against the standards. It is quite possible that they will become more common, given the 1994 requirement for knowledge and understanding to be assessed separately.

A record of oral questioning from an assessor, including answers

The assessor can, and should, ask questions in order to clarify pieces of evidence submitted, or to gain information on areas that don't seem to be covered adequately in the evidence submitted. The onus is on the assessor to write up the questions and answers, and to ensure that they are incorporated in the portfolio.

Contextualizing evidence

This comprises the personal reports, narrative accounts and storyboards referred to earlier in this chapter, which demonstrate knowledge and understanding and the cognitive skills associated with critical reflection.

Historical evidence

Letters of validation from previous employers

These take the form of references that X was in a particular job at a particular time and carried out Y activities to an acceptable standard. They are of limited value.

Certification from other sources

This consists of formal qualifications taken at some point of time in the past. Unless the standards are addressed specifically, it can be of limited value. The candidate should provide examples of syllabuses associated with the qualification and assessments undertaken. It is up to the candidate to contextualize what was covered against the standards.

The issue of how far back one can go with historical evidence is addressed elsewhere (see Chapter 13).

Practical steps that can be taken by providers to support candidates

The following steps should be undertaken by providers:

- Ensure that candidates are given a copy of the awarding body guidelines at the earliest opportunity.
- Check with individual candidates their understanding of the requirements of the awarding body in terms of putting the portfolio together.
- Explain either on a one-to-one basis or through an introductory programme:
  - (a) the differences between candidate-led and assessor-led portfolios;
  - (b) the different types of evidence that can be incorporated;
  - (c) the importance of contextualizing evidence;
  - (d) the importance of an evidence matrix and how this should be put together; and
  - (e) the value of broad-based evidence that avoids relying on a 'filing-cabinet' mentality.
- Show examples of portfolios produced by previous candidates to provide something concrete to work from.
- Develop support networks between candidates, so that each candidate can see how others are going about the collection of evidence.
- Encourage candidates to obtain a workplace mentor and ensure that the mentor has a clear picture of what is expected of candidates (see Chapter 16).

- Arrange a workplace assessment visit with each candidate at an appropriate stage in the programme to try to speed up the evidence-collection process and reduce the volume of material required for the final portfolio (see Chapter 15).
- Consider the use of integrating assignments which encourage candidates to produce performance evidence across a range of elements. Build into the assignments an evaluative element.

References

1 Debling G. and Stuart D. (1992) *Analysing and Minimising the Cost of Assessment, (Competence and Assessment No. 18)*, Employment Department.
2 *National Standards for Assessment and Verification*, Training and Development Lead Body, August 1994.
3 *NVQ Criteria and Guidance*, NCVQ, January 1995.
4 *Implementing the National Standards for Assessment and Verification*, NCVQ, February 1994.
5 *Personal Development and Assessment Guide*, IPD, 1995.
6 MCI, 1990.
7 *The Assessment of Management Competencies*, BTEC/CNAA, 1990.

15 Workplace assessment

Objectives

By the end of this chapter you should be able to:

1 Distinguish between work-based assessment and workplace assessment.
2 Differentiate between different approaches to workplace assessment.
3 Establish the case, or otherwise, for direct observation of a candidate's performance at the workplace.
4 Determine whether at the higher levels workplace assessment should be conducted by internal or external assessors.
5 Understand the value of a work visit by an external assessor, and know how such a visit may be effectively conducted.

Introduction

This chapter is concerned with providing guidelines for assessors of higher level NVQs on how to conduct assessment in the workplace. Given the emphasis that has been placed by proponents of NVQs on the primacy of work-based evidence, this would seem to be a significant feature of the assessor's role. However, as we shall see, it has been the subject of much debate, and there has even been a significant school of thought which has contended that for higher level NVQs, especially in the management area, assessing in the workplace might be inappropriate.

It is argued that, compared to lower level NVQs, there is a decreasing role for workplace observation of an individual's performance in many of the higher level NVQs which have come on-stream. It is maintained, however, that there is considerable scope for a work visit by an external assessor. Guidelines are then provided on how such a work visit may be conducted.

What does assessing in the workplace actually mean?

The first issue is to gain a common understanding as to what assessing in the workplace actually means.

An essential distinction to make is between workplace assessment and work-based assessment.

- *Workplace assessment* is assessment conducted at a candidate's place of work.
- *Work-based assessment* is making judgments about a candidate's performance based on evidence derived from the workplace. Such evidence may be brought by the candidate to the assessor without the assessor ever seeing the workplace.

As we shall see it is not an NVQ requirement that the assessor sees the candidate's workplace, although many authorities have argued that it should be.

In an early (1988) study, Mitchell (1) found that people talked about assessment in the workplace and work-based competence interchangeably, with no common agreement on the use of the terms or no clear understanding of what was being discussed. She goes on to make a set of clarifying distinctions, which relate to assessment in general. Her first relates to whether the assessment takes place within the normal work process, and thus utilizing 'naturally occurring behaviour', or whether it elicits behaviour specifically for assessment purposes. She implies that much of the latter would not take place in the work environment, although special projects and work-related investigations have been used by a number of assessment centres to enable candidates to generate additional evidence.

She then distinguishes between a practical demonstration of a competence, and a cognitive (written or oral) representation of the competence, where the candidate writes or talks about what they would do in a particular situation.

Her third major distinction governs whether the assessment is made on the product of an activity (such as a report) or is undertaken throughout the time the candidate is performing the competence. She argues that: 'generally it will be more cost-effective and as valid, if competence can be safely inferred from the product.'

She also differentiates between internal and external assessors. This chapter will focus on the workplace assessment activities of external assessors, an internal assessor being someone from the candidate's workplace.

Mitchell's distinctions

- Assessment using naturally occuring evidence vs assessment eliciting behaviour specifically for assessment purposes.
- Practical demonstration of a competence vs cognitive (written or oral) demonstration of a competence.

> - Assessment on the product of an activity vs assessment throughout the time the candidate is performing the competence.
> - Assessment by internal assessors vs assessment by external assessors.

Gealy et al. (2) suggest that there are four basic sources of evidence available to assessors to show that candidates can perform an activity described in an NVQ element to the standard defined. These can be cross-referenced to the Mitchell classification:

- Performance at work. They indicate that one form of assessment of this category will be observation of the activities as they occur and checking of the outcomes. This would be a 'practical demonstration' of 'naturally occurring behaviour' using Mitchell's terminology. Another form of evidence within this category would be product evidence, such as a report.
- Performance on specifically set tasks such as projects or assignments. This would elicit 'behaviour specifically for assessment purposes', again following Mitchell.
- Questioning. This would elicit a 'cognitive (written or oral) representation of the competence' (following Mitchell), where the candidate writes or talks about what they would do in a specific situation.
- Historical evidence arising from activities which the candidate has undertaken in the past, either at work or elsewhere. This would include product evidence.

Gealy et al. contend that: 'all of the sources of evidence can be used. In most assessment systems it will probably be wise to use more than one of them, offsetting the strengths of one source of evidence against the weakness of another.'

How can assessment of workplace performance be conducted?

Given the importance of assessing workplace performance, the question becomes: How can this be conducted? Should the onus be on candidates bringing product evidence to an assessor? Or should an assessor

1 Visit a candidate at the workplace, *and*
2 As part of a visit observe a candidate engaging in activities at the workplace?

3 *Or* use the visit primarily to observe products of a candidate's activity in their 'naturally occuring environment'?
4 *Or* be someone from the candidate's workplace?

(1) and (2) are quite different activities for an assessor. Visiting a candidate at the workplace provides an opportunity for an external assessor to establish the nature of the working environment under which he or she has to operate. Observing a candidate undertaking an activity can be an extension of a workplace visit, but is not necessarily entailed in making the visit.

Work-placed observation is always time-consuming and expensive for an external assessor. Nevertheless, at the higher levels, it may be preferable to relying on an internal assessor. For an internal assessor who is not in a line-management relationship with the candidate, it can become problematic at the higher levels to make judgments about the competence of individuals with whom one is working on a day-to-day basis. Such candidates may also possibly be more senior than the assessor.

Gealy et al. (2) suggest that observation of performance at work almost certainly has to be undertaken by the candidate's supervisors or immediate managers. These, they feel, are likely to be the only people who can, and will, keep a close enough eye on the candidate's progress.

This interpretation, however, can create major problems at the higher levels, not least because of the possible power dynamics associated with the seniority of both the proposed assessor and the person being assessed. It also assumes that candidates should be 'kept an eye on', a perspective which is not in keeping with contemporary approaches arguing for greater managerial autonomy. The February 1995 Management Charter Initiative (MCI) Briefing Paper (3) dealing with Management Standards review referred to a number of criticisms being voiced about the Management Standards. One of these was that they do not reflect the reduction in internal-line authority and would benefit from a reduction in terms like 'control', 'subordinate' and 'immediate manager'.

The rest of this chapter is concerned with how, at the higher levels, we can use an external work visit to assess evidence from the workplace using all the categories developed by Gealy et al. This is in the context of National Council for Vocational Qualifications (NCVQ) statements on the primacy of workplace evidence.

Should the visit include observation of an activity?

Gealy et al. (2) develop their explanation of 'performance at work' assessment. They contend that, since occupational competence is defined as the ability to perform the activities required in an occupational area to the standards expected in employment, it follows, logically, that the best evidence of an individual's competence is that generated through performance at work. They are even more specific. They state that direct observation of activity-based performance at work is usually the measure against which other methods are evaluated. This evidence is the only type that takes into account both the time pressures and the pressures from interpersonal relationships which can interfere with performance. Assessment can be unobtrusive, and the conditions are close to the reality of work. Extra pressures may arise, but only because candidates know they are being assessed.

Black (4) argues even more strongly for workplace observation of performance. He states that it is a guiding principle about evidence that, wherever possible, it should be drawn from performance in the workplace – which he goes on to make clear entails for him observation in the workplace. He further argues that 'if other considerations such as time and cost did not have to be taken into account, actual performance in the workplace would arguably be the only appropriate evidence to use'.

Workplace assessment and NCVQ guidelines

It is interesting to compare such statements against NCVQ published guidelines. The January 1995 *NVQ Criteria and Guidance* (5) states that:

NVQs are workbased qualifications, and much of the evidence required for assessment arises from workplace performance. (5: p. 5)

However, the published guidelines have always been a bit confusing about how workplace performance should be assessed.

Thus the March 1991 *Criteria for National Vocational Qualifications* (6) states that:

performance must be demonstrated and assessed under conditions as close as possible to those under which it would normally be practised – preferably in the workplace. (6: p. 21)

Other forms of evidence and assessment are permitted, but it is signalled very strongly that these are second best:

. . . if assessment in the workplace is not practicable, simulations, tests, projects or assignments may provide suitable evidence – but care must be taken to ensure that all elements and performance criteria have been covered, and that it is possible to predict that the competence assessed can be sustained in employment. (6: pp. 21, 23)

This would seem to indicate that some form of workplace visit would be desirable, recognizing that there may be practical difficulties – which are left unspecified.

The 1995 guide makes some subtle changes in wording

... performance must be demonstrated and assessed under conditions which allow accurate assessment of competence to the standard expected in employment – with evidence preferably derived from the workplace. (5: p. 29)

On the surface, this would seem to be a softening of the 1991 position. For me there is a clear difference between the requirement to be assessed 'as close to the workplace situation as possible' and 'to the standard expected in employment'. And 'from the workplace' has a different connotation to 'in the workplace'. An interpretation of 'from the workplace' could be that a given candidate can bring products of workplace activity to the assessor and not require a workplace visit, even if this were possible to arrange.

However, the 1995 guide goes on to say:

... if assessment in the workplace is not practicable, alternative forms of performance evidence may be provided; for example from simulations or projects. (5: p. 29)

This would seem to be sticking to the 1991 rubric recommending workplace visits if possible. All in all, I find the criteria to be ambiguous. I suspect it is because the NCVQ does not wish to be too prescriptive lest they disadvantage candidates who may be unemployed, or otherwise do not have work roles which enable them to generate sufficient workplace evidence. Also, they may well have been influenced by arguments relating to the cost of workplace assessment.

The clearest statement from the NCVQ on the difference between 'product' and 'process' evidence comes from the February 1994 leaflet *Implementing the National Standards for Assessment and Verification.* (7: p. 2):

- 'Product' evidence is likely to be assessed by examining the product itself or a copy of it.
- 'Process' evidence is often best assessed by 'observation' of the process by the assessor. This 'observation' could be from video or audio tapes of the process.

This 1994 paper goes on to make a case for 'candidate-led' portfolios at the higher levels, where the emphasis is on product evidence:

A candidate-led portfolio approach of this kind can be particularly appropriate in collecting a variety of forms of evidence where direct observation of candidates' performance by an assessor is not easily accessible.

It is particularly appropriate for managerial standards.

However, the NVQ guide of 1994 (7) emphasizes that other approaches to evidence collection can be equally valid as opposed to relying only on candidate-led portfolios:

For example, observation of performance by an assessor, supplemented by one-to-one questioning, may be an equally valid way of collecting evidence of competence. The assessor's records of these observations and of the candidate's answers to questions would form an equally valid 'portfolio'.
This type of assessor-led approach does, however, have cost implications in terms of assessor time and may encourage only minimal candidate involvement. (7: p. 4)

The NVQ guidelines seem to discourage an undue emphasis on assessor-led approaches. However, it can form a very important extra set of evidence and corroborations to the candidate-led model. A candidate visit can also speed up the process of evidence gathering by short circuiting elaborate narrative accounts.

Confirmation of the softening of the NVQ rubric on workplace assessment is provided by the revised 1994 TDLB D Units (8). An earlier reference to D32 in *National Standards for Assessment and Verification* (9) referred to it as providing the standards for 'front-line' assessors. It went on to state that the unit assumes that assessment takes place 'locally', primarily through observation of performance and examination of the outcomes of such performance, supported by questioning to assess underpinning knowledge and understanding. The Institute of Training and Development *Assessor and Verifier Award Booklet* (10) interpreted the front-line assessor role as being a workplace assessor, normally a supervisor or manager in the workplace. Essentially this would be someone who is in daily contact with the individual being assessed and therefore can assess on a continuous basis.

The 1994 guidelines for D32 state that the unit could be achieved by assessing a candidate's performance 'under realistic conditions' either in the workplace, or in a training centre or in a college.

In general, the D Unit guidelines are remarkably unhelpful on the subject of workplace assessment. Take D33, for example. D332 is concerned with assessing candidates using different sources of evidence. The range statement refers to evidence derived from natural performance. And that is about it! The knowledge evidence required of an assessor includes statements such as:

... ways of checking the validity and authenticity of evidence, particularly product evidence ...

... how to collect evidence unobtrusively by observation ...

but nothing on how to conduct a workplace visit/assessment or even on how to decide whether or not a workplace visit/assessment is appropriate. The guidance notes for assessors of the unit state that performance evidence for each element of competence should normally be derived from real assessment environments, but then goes silent on what these might be. Given the importance that has been attached by NCVQ to workplace assessment, this seems to me to be very curious.

Fortunately, some of the occupational standards give quite clear guidelines as to the nature of the assessment activities which they feel should be undertaken. The MCI guidelines are particularly helpful.

Workplace assessment and the professions

It has not been common in management circles for work-based visits to be part of a qualification requirement. Some individual tutors have met their students at the student's workplace to discuss projects which have been part of the qualification, but this has not been that usual. However, some professions insist on workplace visits and observations as part of the qualification. It is a requirement for social work and for teaching certificates, for example.

Eraut and Cole (11) summarize the findings of a research project funded by the Employment Department into the professions. They found that direct observation of candidates' performance in the workplace was a key feature of a number of professional routes to accreditation. Of eleven professional groups surveyed, this was an assessment feature of:

- Architecture.
- Surveying.
- Civil engineering.
- Electrical engineering.
- Nursing.
- Optometry.
- Social work.
- Teaching in Scotland (their survey didn't include teaching in England).

It was not an assessment feature of management accountancy and personnel management.

They identified three patterns of assessment of workplace competence:

- During a period of practical experience subsequent to completion of an academic qualification in higher education.
- As an integral part of the academic qualification which then leads directly to professional recognition.
- Conducted both within the academic course and during a subsequent period of professional preparation.

They contend that, for many types of competence, direct observation is the most valid and sometimes the only acceptable method of collecting evidence. In most cases this is accompanied by some kind of informal questioning of the candidates to discover their analysis of the task or situation, their reasons for their actions and their evaluation of what occurred. Sometimes this is extended to questioning clients or other people present. Questioning of candidates may also be used to extend the range of the evidence collected by asking about what they would have done if certain things had happened or if certain features of the situation had been different.

When an appropriate assessor is frequently present to observe performance and question the candidate, it is relatively easy for assessor training to ensure that a proper sample is used. But this becomes more difficult when special arrangements have to be made for an assessor to be present. In such circumstances, practicality and cost will restrict observation to a small sample of behaviour and the possibility of an observer effect will have to be considered. When work has to be reorganized to ensure that particular things happen when an assessor is visiting, we are moving towards 'simplified practice' rather than 'natural observation'.

Eraut and Cole (11) also suggest that assessment procedures are rather patchy for workplace assessment. Although most professions provide some training for assessors, several lack explicit criteria for assessment in the workplace. While it may seem reasonable to claim that assessments made by experienced practitioners have a degree of validity, the lack of explicit criteria and/or verification procedures weakens their public accountability.

Workplace assessment not relying on observation of an activity

However, at the higher levels within organizations, direct workplace assessment of an activity becomes increasingly problematic. As one progresses up the NVQ levels, the type of roles people undertake, and the activities in which they are involved are increasingly less susceptible to observation of workplace activity. Many activities consist of processes taking place over a considerable amount of time. The development of a new quality-control system can entail months of investigation, analysis, negotiation for resources and development of implementation schedules. One can, however, gain sight of the products of a range of activities. Such products are often documents and reports – or even refurbishments of buildings that a manager has commissioned. The activities are often the outcomes of considerable reflection and are not time bound in the sense that one can observe a candidate undertaking an activity.

Workplace assessment and the management standards

The assessment of the national standards for management is a case in point. The 1990 MCI guidance booklet on assessment (12) is based on the assumption that:

... management standards do not call for a strong focus on direct observation.

Only 20 per cent of the MII standards have direct observation listed as a form of evidence.

This 20 per cent can be broken down into seven elements within the Management II standards where observation is listed as being a feasible proposition. Of these, only two seem to be observation of an activity as opposed to a product. The two examples of observation of an activity are:

- Create and maintain the necessary conditions for productive work activity. These relate to the element 'Set and update work objectives for teams and individuals'. As an assessor, I am not at all clear how an event could be set up at the workplace that would be sufficiently realistic and natural for me to be convinced that the standard was being met.
- The second example relates to the element 'Negotiate and agree budgets'. I suspect that very few employers would allow such negotiations to be open to external inspection.

The 1990 MCI guidance argues that managerial roles provide particular challenges for assessment. Compared to activities undertaken for awards at NVQ levels 1–3, in management there is often greater independence of action, less supervision and a significant personal performance role. Judgments are rarely clear-cut. The critical impact of a management decision is often difficult to attribute to a given individual because of time lag.

In terms of performance at work, following the Gealy et al. (2) classification, the 1990 MCI booklet contends that, in addition to

- Products of the manager's daily work (e.g. reports, production schedules, proposals, balance sheets, articles, letters).

and

- Observation (specifically for assessment purposes by line manager or assessor or someone acting on the assessor's behalf).

evidence from performance at work can take the form of

- Witness testimony (oral or written from a variety of reliable individuals who have contact with the work of the candidate, e.g. colleagues, line-manager, subordinates, customers).
- Personal report (a description of the actions that have or would have to be taken). MCI recommend personal reports to cover much of the interpersonal skills, etc., associated with the manager's role.

Many time-bound activities such as disciplinary interviews are not only confidential, but entail prior preparation, investigation, etc., that would be too time-consuming for an assessor to observe even if the confidentiality and delicate nature of the investigation didn't intervene.

Conducting the work visit

The SCOTVEC model

SCOTVEC (13) make the following practical observations in respect of workplace visits.

Planning for the candidate's assessment should address the following practical issues:

- The number and dates of assessment visits (dates should be negotiated with the candidate, in discussion with the mentor and the assessor, and should be arranged to allow the candidate the greatest opportunity to demonstrate competence).
- The availability of the candidate, the assessor and others involved in the assessment process, for the assessment visit.
- The provision of necessary resources and equipment for the assessment visit.
- The administrative requirements for the assessment visit, such as the provision of the necessary documentation for recording the candidate's achievement.
- The collection of evidence before the assessment visit, if appropriate, in order to provide the assessor with different types of evidence, and sufficient evidence, to allow an assessment judgment to be made.

This part of the process is vital – the candidate should have in mind the sort of documentary evidence, or indeed physical evidence, that can be presented against a given element/unit. However, I have found that by dint of careful questioning one can often discover suitable and sufficient evidence that the candidate had not considered – merely by virtue of my greater familiarity with the standards.

SCOTVEC refer to all this in the context of 'visiting assessors'. It is a bit unclear in their guidelines how the role of the visiting assessor differs from a tutor operating both as the assessor and also being responsible for other aspects of the candidate's development. The visiting assessor is classified as a 'peripatetic assessor' and is defined as someone who is not in day-to-day contact with the candidate but who visits at a prearranged time to carry out the assessment. Their use enables centres which do not have suitably qualified assessors at sites on which assessments are taking place to provide assessment opportunities for candidates. This is a conventional assessment approach for colleges and other approved centres for whom candidates can come from a wide array of organizational backgrounds.

The way forward

The question becomes: 'Is workplace assessment worth conducting for senior management roles, given the cost and the alternative forms of evidence listed?'

In my opinion a work visit can be an invaluable part of both the assessment and the support process. If all the evidence is based on portfolios then it can, in theory, preclude the need for a work-based visit and direct observation. My experience as an assessor is that a work visit is a vital part of the assessment procedure and should be encouraged. It is not so much that at the higher NVQ levels one can observe a candidate in action. It is rather that one can authenticate the environment in which a candidate purports to operate. One can see the filing systems and safety procedures in situ. And one can facilitate, by being there, the production of evidence. I have found that questions asked while one is with a candidate at his or her workplace can generate information which would not otherwise come to light. The 'Ah, perhaps this report might be helpful' response is typical. Also, by physically seeing some reports taken from filing cabinets and elsewhere, one can speed up the accreditation process, give the candidate confidence that he or she is on the right lines, and reduce the sheer volume of documentary evidence that might otherwise be required for the finished portfolio.

The workplace visit can combine three forms of evidence demonstration:

- Observation (although not necessarily of an activity).
- Product evidence.
- Questioning.

However, one is not conducting the visit to observe the candidate engaging in activities, which as we have seen are difficult to set up, and can be artificial and based on simplified practice rather than naturally occurring evidence. Rather, it is to see products of candidates' activity in the work setting. Products could include:

- The work environment itself (equipment, space, rooms, filing systems, IT systems).
- Reports, contract data and other relevant documentary evidence.

The visit should consist of candidates producing documentary and other evidence relating to elements and units against which they feel they might be able to claim credit. By being in the work environment, a skilled and knowledgeable assessor can ask questions which lead candidates to produce evidence and to provide supporting explanations for units which, without the visit, they might not have felt possible to claim any credit. Almost without exception a candidate has said to me 'I would never have thought of that' or 'I have done X – see this report – is that suitable evidence?' – invariably it is.

The workplace visit can corroborate much of the documentary evidence. One can see whether the environment is a safe place in which to operate. One can see whether information is stored systematically and securely. One can see what information technology is available and how it is being used.

One does not just passively observe during a workplace visit. Throughout one should ask a candidate for clarifying information. Most of what one gets access to is product evidence such as reports and documents. Many of these can emerge as the result of questioning e.g. 'Have you ever had to do X?' or 'How did you set about it?' This line of questioning could, of course, be undertaken away from the workplace, but it is amazing how often a candidate can access there and then reports and supporting documentation from files which, away from the workplace, would not be available.

It is important during a workplace visit to write detailed notes of the evidence one has seen and what one has heard and the elements, units and performance criteria to which it relates. I find that I am able to provisionally accredit a number of units on the basis of what I have seen and elicited through questioning. Where this is the case I make a statement to that effect, e.g. 'Happy to accredit', and inform the candidate orally of this. I would expect the candidate to take a copy of my handwritten notes, type them up and incorporate them in the final portfolio after I have signed to say that the typed version is an accurate record. If

I have seen the documentary evidence I would recommend that candidates only provide a sample in the final portfolio, in order to avoid the final portfolio being top heavy.

I would expect the candidate to prepare for the visit. They should have available for me any documentary or other supporting evidence for any element/unit against which they feel they have engaged in relevant activity. I would always cross-examine them on the evidence presented and on their role in the process, and record their answers. Normally, I would attempt to undertake the assessment in unit sequence as presented in the standards. This I find easier to record.

An assessment activity of this sort takes three to six hours, depending on the quality of the information and the degree of preparedness of the candidate. Invariably, candidates find it a most valuable and supportive experience. It can take a great weight off their minds to suddenly discover that they have evidence against a unit which they hadn't previously thought of.

It clearly helps if the candidate is fully familiar with the standards. It is vital that the assessor knows the standards inside out and also has a full grasp of the field.

The timing of the workplace assessment visit is important to determine. I would recommend that an activity of this kind takes place towards the end of a development programme when the candidate is assembling the portfolio. It is at this stage that the candidate has greatest familiarity with the standards and has a clearer feel of the product evidence that can be presented and which standards it relates to.

Extract from notes taken on a work visit

Accreditation process conducted by John Walton with Tim W. for MCI II

MCI II Element 1.1

Tim showed me work done on Counselling Skills programme. Included a statement on equipment requirements, and a timetable, and supporting materials and a set of tutor notes. All in a bound and indexed folder.

Saw project meeting notes from the briefing day Tim set up to review and update materials and strategy.

Saw papers on similar exercise conducted for Interpersonal Communications programme.

These included need to identify appropriate tutors – who were then recruited by Tim.

The programme was resourced on the assumption that there would be twelve delegates and two tutors.

A break-even analysis was done per course. Tim gave an example of one tutor dropping out because numbers were low.
Example also given of internal resourcing of programmes to cut costs.
Courses were monitored with programme managers' meetings to ensure not running at a loss (programme viability).
Evaluation sheets always collected and summarized.
Tim showed me summary sheets of course evaluations and tutor sheets which he then took action on.
Monthly report to management team was seen which showed trends, e.g. decline in numbers.
Happy to accredit performance evidence.

References

1 Mitchell L. (1988) *Assessing Occupational Competence – What Does it Mean in Practice? (Competence and Assessment No. 2)* Employment Department.
2 Gealy et al. Designing assessment systems for national certification. In: *Development of Assessable Standards for National Certification* (ed. Fennell E.), Employment Department.
3 *Management Standards Review – Briefing Paper*, MCI, February 1995.
4 Black H. (1992) *Sufficiency of Evidence (Competence and Assessment No. 20)*, Employment Department.
5 *NVQ Criteria and Guidance*, NCVQ, January 1995.
6 *Criteria for National Vocational Qualifications*, NCVQ, March 1991.
7 *Implementing the National Standards for Assessment and Verification*, NCVQ, February 1994.
8 *National Standards for Assessment and Verification*, TDLB, August 1994.
9 *National Standards for Assessment and Verification (NCVQ Report No. 13)*, NCVQ, 1991.
10 *Assessor and Verifier Award Booklet*, Institute of Training and Development, 1992.
11 Eraut M. and Cole G. (1993) *Assessment of Competence in Higher Level Occupations (Competence and Assessment No. 21)*, Employment Department.
12 *Assessment Guidelines*, MCI, 1990.
13 *Guide to Assessment*, SCOTVEC, October 1993.

16 Mentoring

Objectives

By the end of this chapter you should be able to:

1 Describe in general terms the role of a mentor.
2 Establish the importance of the mentor in an NVQ programme.
3 Specify the role of a mentor in assessing NVQs.
4 Clarify the relationship between mentor and providing centre.
5 Develop guidelines for training of mentors.

Introduction

In *The Odyssey*, Homer talks of Mentor, the faithful retainer of Ulysseus, to whom was entrusted the care of his young son Telemachus, until the wanderer returned. The word 'mentor' has been taken into organizational practice to refer to experienced and often senior employees who support and guide less experienced and often younger colleagues through their personal and career development.

Collin (1) in her chapter on learning and development provides a useful summary from the literature of four general requirements for effective mentoring:

- *The status and characteristics of the mentor*. Factors listed include:
  (a) need for seniority and standing within a given organization,
  (b) absence of line management relationship with mentoree or protégé,
  (c) good 'people-developing' skills, and
  (d) ability to learn from the protégé.
- *The protégé*. Factors listed include:
  (a) possession of potential, and
  (b) desire to learn and develop in order to realize potential.
- *The relationship*. Factors listed include:
  (a) should be based on mutual trust, and
  (b) development over time, possibly into full friendship.
- *The activities*. Factors listed include:
  (a) mentor acting as role model, and
  (b) mentor providing support and encouragement.

Collin argues that not everyone is capable of carrying out these roles and that there needs to be some careful selection of mentors.

The role of mentor is also seen by many awarding bodies as one of the key support functions for candidates undertaking NVQ programmes.

While, as we shall see, there is much agreement on the above general requirements for effective mentoring, there are different schools of thought on issues such as:

- The scope of the mentoring role. For example, should the mentor be involved in assessment?
- Should the mentor come from the candidate's own organization or not?
- Should the centre or the candidate be responsible for finding a mentor?

Scope of mentoring role

There is a general consensus on:

- The basis of the mentor – candidate relationship.
- The core skills a mentor should possess.
- Activities that a mentor should undertake.

The 1990 Council for National Academic Awards (CNAA)/BTEC joint publication *The Assessment of Management Competences* (2) argues that mentors should support and guide the work-based components of candidate's learning. They should also facilitate access to the necessary resources and information required for the completion of tasks necessary to demonstrate competence. It is suggested that there should be quite a close tripartite relationship between the principal participants of tutor, candidate and mentor. Mentors working alongside a course team may well be also involved in assessment.

The Institute of Management (IM) have an established mentor system for candidates for their programmes. They believe that the mentor has a major role to play in the development of the candidate. The students' guide to the IM's Certificate in Management programme states that the principal objectives of an IM mentor are to promote the circumstances by which candidates can gain the confidence, skills, attitudes and opportunities to manage and develop their own learning.

The major task of the IM mentors is to guide and support candidates throughout their training towards becoming a competent manager. Through developing a close relationship with the candidate, by holding regular meetings to review the candidate's portfolio, the mentor can provide discrete tuition and guidance, which will give invaluable feedback to the candidate, the organization and the awarding body. In order to do this, mentors might be involved in a number of roles at various times:

- Coach.
- Facilitator or creative problem-solver.
- Counsellor.
- Advisor/guide.
- Co-ordinator.
- Assessor (where the mentor acts as assessor, specific training to defined national standards will be required).
- Role model.
- Confidant.
- Communicator.
- Bridge/link (including to the Institute and the line manager).
- Partner.
- Friend.

Candidates are informed that they can expect that their mentors will:

- Help them to set learning objectives.
- Know the requirements of the programme, and gain support within a candidate's organization so that these requirements can be met.
- Help candidates structure their learning programme and manage their time.
- Help solve problems and create opportunities.
- Give constructive and assertive feedback.
- Advise about evidence and assessment.
- Supervise candidates throughout the learning process leading to an award.

Mentors will be more experienced as managers than will candidates and will have specialist functional and technical skills which can be drawn upon. Candidates, however, should not expect mentors to be an expert on every possible subject. But they are likely to have influence within a candidate's organization and should be the route to obtaining the help and expertise needed.

Note that the mentoring relationship can be long term and not just restricted to portfolio development.

It is unwise for one individual to take on too many protégés; Geiger Dumond and Boyle (3) recommend two as a maximum.

Using a similar classification to the IM, Leibowitz and Schlossberg (4) develop some of the roles for mentors.

Roles for mentors

Communicator

- Encourages two-way exchange of information.
- Acts as a sounding board for ideas and concerns.
- Schedules uninterrupted time to meet with mentoree.

Counsellor

- Helps mentoree plan strategies to achieve mutually agreed upon personal goals.

Coach

- Helps to clarify performance goals and development needs.
- Reinforces effective on-the-job performance.
- Recommends specific behaviours in which the mentoree needs improvement.
- Serves as a role model to demonstrate successful professional behaviour.

Advisor

- Recommends training opportunities from which the mentoree could benefit.
- Reviews the mentoree's development plan on a regular basis.

Broker (bridge/link in IM terms)

- Helps the mentoree identify resources.
- Expands the mentoree's network of professional contacts.
- Helps link mentorees with appropriate employment opportunities.

Referral agent

- Identifies resources to help the mentoree with specific problems.
- Follows up to ensure that the referred resources were useful.

Advocate

- Intervenes on the mentoree's behalf, representing the mentoree's concerns to higher level management for redress on specific issues.

Characteristics of good mentors

According to the 1990 CNAA/BTEC publication, good mentors are, in general:

- Confident and perceptive of their own position in the organization and do not feel threatened by, or resentful of, the candidate's opportunities.
- Sufficiently senior to be well informed about the organization and able to facilitate the candidate's opportunities.
- Knowledgeable about the candidate's area of interest, thus complementing the more general role of the tutor.
- Supportive of the objective of the programme and perceive, and are committed to fulfil, their own particular responsibilities to the candidate.
- Easily accessible to the candidate and willing to negotiate a planned timetable with candidate and tutor.
- Already in a positive professional relationship with the candidate.
- Treating their mentoring role as an integral part of their own job responsibilities, not as an add on.

Peer mentoring

Most of these conditions would also apply where the mentor is a peer rather than a superior in the same organizational hierarchy. However, under these circumstances the role is more likely to be a reflective partnership and mentoring a reciprocal supportive relationship between two candidates who can draw on their own network for resources. For example, candidates with similar posts of responsibility in different branches of the same organization could fulfil a mutual counselling role. Such a mutual support relationship could prove to be of significant advantage to both candidates in sustaining momentum and helping each other to identify and get together evidence for the portfolio.

The role of the mentor in assessment

The IM position is that, in conjunction with an assessor, the mentor should endorse a candidate's portfolio. This perspective is not universally held and many authorities on the subject do not include any assessment role within the relationship.

The 1990 CNAA/BTEC publication (2) goes on to suggest that being a mentor is not an easy task, and yet adequate support from a workplace is a crucial element in a candidate's success. It is important to distinguish the mentor function from assessment and from executive responsibility such as is incurred when a line manager is also a mentor. When the same person is fulfilling both mentoring and an assessment role, providers will need to be satisfied that the assessment is being conducted in a fair and rigorous way and that the candidate is also receiving adequate support in preparation for assessment.

Relationship between centre and mentor

A number of centres have no relationship whatsoever with mentors, sometimes leaving it entirely in the hands of candidates as to whether they obtain mentors or not. Such a hands-off arrangement is not good practice. Experience indicates that without some support from the centre, the candidate–mentor relationship often fails. On the other hand, some centres – and indeed awarding bodies – can be very prescriptive about their relationship with the mentor.

According to SCOTVEC (5), the centre should select the duties to be performed by a particular mentor in any given situation. Having decided on the most appropriate combination, the centre should then normally record the duties of the mentor in writing. The three main duties they identify for mentors are to give *advice and support* to candidates, to help to *collect evidence* and to provide *authentication*. These three functions can be exercised together or singly by a mentor, depending on the kind of mentor that the candidate requires or the award demands.

The SCOTVEC Guide develops these three duties:

- *Advising* involves an experienced practitioner guiding and supporting the candidate as he or she undertakes an award.
- *Collecting evidence* involves assisting the candidate with portfolio production and gathering evidence of the candidate's competence in formative assessment activities and retaining this evidence for the assessor.
- *Authenticating* involves confirming that an activity, task or exercise has been carried out by the candidate and that the rules governing the assessment of that activity have been followed.

This concept of the mentor role is similar to that of 'personal development adviser' referred to by the Institute of Personnel and Development (IPD) in their student packs for NVQ qualifications in T&D. However, the IPD distinguishes between the role of personnel development adviser and that of mentor. Mentor they see as being restricted to a member of staff from the candidate's own organization. The personal development adviser they define as the person who can guide and support candidates through the process of development and assessment. He or she can work in close partnership with candidates and candidates' organizations, and will have a commitment to a given candidate and his or her achievement.

The adviser will work with a group of trainers or managers from an approved assessment centre. It is one of the responsibilities of the personal development adviser to provide a constant support role throughout the development of the learner. Ways in which the adviser can assist include:

- Negotiating his or her availability to candidates at times and places suited to the candidate's development needs.
- Liaising with the candidate's employer or organization.
- Providing appropriate support leading to an impartial needs analysis.
- Interpreting the standards.
- Providing information, advice and guidance about methods of learning and the availability of appropriate resources.
- Guiding, advising and arranging assessment of prior learning and achievement of performance evidence.
- Assisting in the preparation of portfolios.

Clearly, there is a lot of overlap between the functions exercised by the personal development advisor and the candidate's mentor. The key difference is that the personal development advisor is a guaranteed source of support to the candidate from the centre.

Responsibility for finding mentors

Many centres and awarding bodies put the onus on the candidate. The IM guidelines argue that the mentor should normally be identified by the candidate. There are significant advantages in the candidate taking on this responsibility. In working towards an NVQ they are undertaking a process where they are going to have to take significant responsibility for their own learning. Unless they are registering with a centre operating within their own organization they have a clearer knowledge than anyone from outside of the likely sources of support. They are also likely to be more committed to a choice they themselves have made.

The 1993 SCOTVEC publication *Guide to Assessment* (5), however, sees the centre as having a key role both in choosing the mentor as well as subsequently allocating duties. This is made clear in the elaboration of the advisory function. In line with other authorities they contend that this is usually carried out by a person who works in the same field as the candidate, but who is not necessarily in close contact with him or her. The mentor who advises should be an experienced practitioner who is seen by the candidate as a role model and who is available to support and help the candidate as he or she progresses through an award. The guide then goes on to say that an example of this function is in management SVQs, where the centre is responsible for appointing a mentor for each candidate undertaking the award.

In my experience, it is difficult for centres to identify suitable mentors for candidates unless the centre is operating within a specific organization. However, the centre can provide guidelines to candidates on the qualities to look for in a mentor, and the ingredients of a successful mentoring arrangement.

Where should the mentor be based?

Many centres encourage candidates to find mentors from their own organization and this relationship is very valuable if a candidate needs to gain work-based support. This approach is based on the view that mentors are, ideally, people placed within a candidate's work organization and who can give both guidance on the construction of their portfolio and also give access to work opportunities.

The IM guidelines state that the mentor is, ideally, a professionally qualified manager, or holds a senior managerial or technical position within the organization. The line manager is often not the most appropriate person. The professional discipline and career path of the mentor should be similar to that being undertaken by the candidate concerned, and it will be an advantage if the mentor is a member or fellow of an appropriate professional body. The mentor must know what the candidate should be doing, be able to give some time to the candidate on a regular basis and be prepared to help the candidate become a manager.

It is possible, however, that a candidate might not be able to obtain a work-based mentor. Some centres, in such circumstances, nominate a centre advisor as mentor – taking on a sort of personal tutor role. It is clearly important that such a nominee is not involved in the assessment process.

The mentoring process

Geiger Dumond and Boyle (3) argue that successful mentoring relationships don't just happen. Even if an organization has a workable mentoring system, the relationship will not be a productive one unless the mentor and mentoree both understand their role. They go on to offer the following guidelines:

- One of the most important aspects of a good mentoring relationship is to meet on a regular basis. This should be at least once a month. A good mentoring relationship cannot be developed if the parties don't get to know each other.

- Be a good listener.
- Do not betray confidences.
- Discuss strengths and development needs with mentorees and provide guidance in developing these areas. Provide feedback on technical and interpersonal competence as perceived by customers and influential decision-makers.

The mentoring process typically starts with the candidate and his or her mentor. They should hold a personal development discussion that covers the candidate's strengths, her or his development needs, specific skills the candidate will work on to develop for the future, and a development plan. Time commitment and joint expectations also need to be discussed. It is difficult for either party to be clear on what is expected unless such matters have been discussed.

There could well be a formal agreement between the candidate and the mentor. Such an agreement could take the form of a document with headings such as the following:

Area of agreement	Substance of agreement
Confidentiality	
Duration of relationship	
Frequency of meetings	
Specific role of mentor	
Specific role of candidate	

Some providers interview prospective mentors, alongside their candidates, in order to optimize mutual understanding and establish guarantees of sustained support throughout the programme and assessment. The 1990 CNAA/BTEC publication (2) recommended that providers formalize arrangements with mentors prior to candidates being accepted on a programme of study, and ensure that members are willing and able to provide the degree of support required for the candidate to be adequately prepared for assessment. Special attention will be necessary for students who are not sponsored by an organization.

Some centres encourage a tripartite agreement between the centre, the candidate and the mentor on such matters as the development plan. However, this can often be no more than a paper exercise unless the centre maintains some contact with mentors.

There is a strong case for getting mentors together so that they can compare experiences and develop a network. Such a process would be easier to organize if candidates and mentors all came from the same organization. In such a case there could well be a mentor co-ordinator. It would also be easier to monitor the effectiveness of the mentor–candidate relationship.

Some organizations give careful attention to the selection of mentors. However, there is a school of thought that the relationship should be a voluntary one and initiated by the candidate.

Training of mentors

There is a strong argument for centres offering training to mentors on a voluntary attendance basis. Some providers of NVQ programmes offer mentor training of up to two days. The programme consists typically of an introduction to:

- NVQs in general.
- Occupational standards in particular.
- The assessment methodology of the centre and awarding body.
- Some of the skills associated with being a mentor.
- Approaches to sustaining commitment within the relationship.
- Styles of mentoring.

There could also be joint training in which both candidates and mentors are given guidance by the centre on how the relationship might be developed and insights into some of the pitfalls that might occur.

Scenario 4

You are the co-ordinator of a college-based NVQ centre. Jane, a candidate for an NVQ at level 4 comes to you and indicates she is having difficulties in getting a mentor within her own organization. On closer questioning, you establish that she is doing the NVQ off her own bat, and that the organization she works for is not really interested in whether she gets the qualification or not. What would you recommend?

For a possible approach see Chapter 17.

References

1 Collin A. (1994) Learning and development. In: *Human Resource Management – A Contemporary Perspective* (eds. Beardwell I. and Holden L.), Pitman, chap. 8.
2 *The Assessment of Management Competencies* BTEC/CNAA, 1990.
3 Geiger-Dumond A. and Boyle S. (1995) *Training and Development*, March.
4 Leibowitz Z. B. and Schlossberg N. K. (1981) *Training and Development Journal*, July.
5 *Guide to Assessment*, SCOTVEC, October 1993.

17 Answers to questions and scenarios

Question 1

The Advanced GNVQ in Management Studies, mentioned earlier in the section, should be generally available from September 1996. You would need to decide which awarding body to go to. Note that there is a much narrower range of approved awarding bodies for GNVQs than for NVQs. Currently they are restricted to the BTEC, the City & Guilds and the RSA Examinations Board.

Remember that each awarding body must offer the eight mandatory units which are part of the qualification as well as the three core skills units. It is worth establishing the differences in the four optional units which are specific to and copyrighted by individual awarding bodies. Another distinguishing feature between awarding bodies will be the additional units on offer.

However, it is worth being clear as to your objectives in offering this particular qualification. Evidence from pilot studies has indicated that the GNVQ is struggling to find its place in the 'market'. There is evidence of some conflict with existing qualifications. You need to be clear in your own mind who you are aiming it at. Is it for 16 to 19-year-olds who are seeking a vocational A level on route to a university degree? Or is it a pre-competence award for individuals seeking to gain access to or to return to job opportunities in the management arena?

Nevertheless, the format of the management GNVQs is simpler and more accessible to candidates than that of associated NVQs, and the evidence indicators are quite straightforward and realistic.

Assuming that you decide to proceed you will need to satisfy certain conditions which will be familiar to those centres who have been involved with NVQs. To be approved as a centre you will need to provide evidence that you understand the requirements of GNVQs are adequately resourced and capable of offering satisfactory courses and are able to carry out assessments to the required standards.

For example, you will need to have in place suitably trained teachers who are qualified to conduct internal assessment of the projects assignments and other activities which students carry out during their course. You will also need trained internal verifiers who will oversee assessment by checking a sample of the students' work, and the associated records to ensure that appropriate standards are being applied.

Considerable planning and staff development are required before starting courses. You will need to:

- Design or select assignments to cover the unit requirements.
- Allow students scope to plan their own work.
- Provide integrated development and assessment of core skills (4: p. 22).

Although it is not a formal GNVQ requirement it is strongly recommended that you provide induction programmes for potential students, so that they become acquainted with the qualifications, the type of work required, the range of units on offer and the grading criteria.

As part of the induction programme students should be encouraged to consider their achievements to date, interests and preferences, career aspirations and learning needs. From this starting point an action plan can be developed (4: p. 23).

Remember that, unlike NVQs, the evidence focus is not on workplace assessment. Instead students will be producing assignments and reports without necessarily being in work.

Question 2

Yes, in principle it is permissible to offer a 'hybrid programme' (see the section on hybrid programmes), but you would need to satisfy a number of conditions for it to be meaningful to candidates. These would include:

- Specifying what standards are being addressed in the programme.
- Clarifying how the course assessment mechanisms contribute to the achievement of the standards.
- Ensuring that the members of the course team who are assessing the work for the academic programme are familiar with the standards and are, ideally, NVQ-assessor accredited.
- Establishing what advice needs to be given to student candidates about how they should get evidence together for NVQ assessment.

You will need to rewrite your course documentation to show which standards are being addressed and how the assessment methods contributed to their demonstration. You would also need to indicate the additional support you intend to give to candidates to enable them to .generate a portfolio of performance evidence.

In practice, to become an NVQ centre you need to satisfy the requirements of the awarding body that you decide to register with. This would include liaising with the external verifier for advice on your proposed approach.

Question 3

The following approaches are recommended:

1 Provide each student-candidate with programme documentation which clearly shows the relationship between taught inputs, learning outcomes, and NVQ standards. Ideally, for each post-graduate unit, you should indicate:

   - What participants should know and be able to explain by the time they have completed their learning.
   - The content (body of knowledge) that will be covered by means of taught inputs, distance learning material, etc.
   - Which NVQ standards will have been addressed.
   - The laid down assessments, how these are contextualized against the standards, and how they will contribute to the final NVQ portfolio of evidence.

2 Provide taught inputs covering the body of knowledge that has been built up over the years in a given topic area before addressing the specifics of NVQ standards. It makes much more sense to individuals if they have a broad-based coverage of topics and themes before they focus on more narrowly defined NVQ elements and performance criteria. It also reduces the likelihood of undue compartmentalization and atomization of thinking and understanding.

3 Ensure that the programme team are totally familiar with the NVQ standards, unit by unit, and element by element.

4 Show how the assignments on the academic programme contribute to NVQ standards. This can be accomplished by the following use of words at the end of the assignment brief: 'This assignment should enable you to generate evidence against the following standards'.

5 Cross-map any assessments which have to be undertaken as part of the programme to NVQ elements and units on a chart (see Figure 17.1) and tick which of the elements are covered by which of the assignments.

6 Recognize that the assignments might not cover all the performance criteria associated with a given element and might only provide supporting and supplementary evidence of competence.

7 At the beginning of the programme, reserve the equivalent of two days to address standards and assessment methodology, how evidence may be generated and how the academic programme supports the NVQ model.

8 Throughout the programme devote chunks of input time explaining and discussing individual standards with student-candidates.

9 Complete 'academic assessment' first – help candidates to fill in NVQ gaps subsequently through them adding to their portfolio.

Assignment	MCI II standard (unit and element)												
	1.1	1.2	1.3	2.1	2.2	2.3	2.4	3.1	3.2	3.3	4.1	4.2	etc.
1													
2													
3													
4													
etc.													

10 On each completed and assessed assignment, get the assessor to endorse which standards have been met. The process can be simplified if you:

- Encourage candidates to list standards claimed in the frontispiece of their assignment, with an indication of where the evidence is to be found.
- Ask assessors to tick (or otherwise) and sign that standards claimed are agreed.
- Ask assessors to make notes on the assessment sheet of any gaps or uncertainties that they have identified.
- Encourage candidates to incorporate product evidence as appendices to assignments to justify claims made in textual narrative. Request that they ensure each piece of product evidence is contextualized and cross-referred to the written text.
- Specify to candidates that they make marginal references in their written assignments to any particular standard addressed.

11 Allocate to each student-candidate a personal advisor from within the programme team, whom they can draw upon for support.

Question 4

The provision of an induction programme is a helpful part of the APL process, unless the candidate is very experienced in NVQ thinking and is particularly self-motivated.

A typical induction process involves:

- An initial assessment/advice session.
- A detailed advisory interview.

- An explanation of APL (perhaps in a workshop setting).
- A workshop on evidence gathering.
- Portfolio-management counselling or workshop sessions.
- The creation of an individual learning contract.

This process would then be followed by tutor/assessor workshops. My experience is that candidates get 'swamped' early on by the sheer mass of information on NVQs being provided and the associated 'technical language' associated with NVQ standards. It is deceptive how many follow-up support sessions can be entailed and this is not always mirrored in the cost charged to candidates.

Scenario 1

Colin would seem to be an ideal candidate to undertake an MCI I qualification. Almost certainly, some of the evidence in his GNVQ portfolio will be relevant to the MCI I award. Evidence from the field is that the Advanced Management GNVQ is, in terms of level, situated somewhere between NVQ level 3 and NVQ level 4. His experience in putting together a portfolio of evidence will be invaluable.

Scenario 2

Assuming that the Diploma in Management Studies (DMS) is a two-year programme, Folashade should have little difficulty getting accepted by most universities – certainly new universities – even though she does not have a first degree. Some universities underpin their DMS with a first-year post-graduate Certificate in Management. Technically, Folashade does not have the academic credits to go straight onto the final second-year stage of a Diploma in Management Studies.

Some universities have linked their post-graduate management awards to the MCI qualifications. This is also possible with the Institute of Management qualifications which have post-graduate credits from the Open University Validation Service.

To go for a linked qualification would seem to be a sensible step for Folashade. Questions to clarify would focus on the extent of organizational support she could expect from her employer in respect of generating evidence for her portfolio.

Scenario 3

It says a lot about the organization culture that Derek has been 'instructed' that he must have an MCI II qualification in two years time. I trust the assessors for the investors-in-people status pick up this attitude to learning and development.

Derek is not being at all realistic. One gets the impression that he feels 'put on' by his employer who is effectively diverting him from his real goal, that of getting an MBA. However, to attempt an APL route for an MCI II award is, as we have seen, not an easy option. In trying for two qualifications he could end up with neither. In my opinion he must choose between either going for an MBA and 'forgetting' about the instruction, or gritting his teeth, deferring the MBA, and undertaking the MCI II qualification through a centre formal-learning programme.

Scenario 4

This is not an uncommon situation. In my experience quite a high percentage of candidates are either self-funded or are in an organization which does not give them support. Despite this, many candidates find that they can identify someone within their organization structure who can provide advice and guidance. Should this not be the case – as for Jane – then you could nominate one of your own centre advisors as mentor. There may well be other candidates who are in a similar position, and an additional approach could be to set up supportive pairing arrangements.

Some awarding bodies have an established network of mentors, and drawing upon this can be an alternative solution. You may also consider setting up your own network of mentors from professionals in the field who see providing such support as part of their continuous professional development.

Index

EFFECTIVE MEASUREMENT & MANAGEMENT OF IT COSTS & BENEFITS

COMPUTER WEEKLY
PROFESSIONAL SERIES

DAN REMENYI, ARTHUR MONEY AND ALAN TWITE

Credit Card Hotline Tel: (01865) 314627

For those concerned with the rocketing level of IT expenditure this book can show you how to take control and make more effective use of IT.

The rapidly increasing expenditure on IT in most organizations is one reason why IT benefits management has become an important concern.

This book provides a basic, practical framework for understanding the economic issues of information as well as some suggestions as to how a company's IT efforts may be appraised.

This book:

- Looks at the IT investment decision process
- Shows how to produce cost/benefits analysis of IT spend
- Shows how to measure benefits and how to evaluate the success of the IT function
- Includes case studies - learn by example

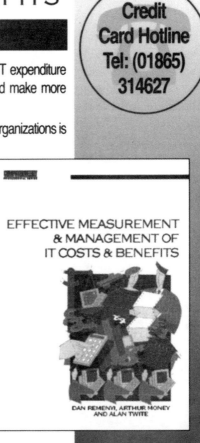

1995, 246 x 189mm, 285 pages, paperback
0 7506 2432 9, £27.49 (price includes postage and packing)

HOW TO ORDER

☎ **Credit Card Hotline**: Tel. (0)1865 314627

✉ **Or send orders to**: Sharon Pitcher, Butterworth-Heinemann, Linacre House, Jordan Hill, Oxford, OX2 8DP quoting ref: T603TCKA01

By cheque or credit card (overseas customers please pay by credit card or a cheque drawn in sterling on a UK bank).

Cheques should be made payable to Heinemann Publishers Oxford Credit Card orders: please state the make of card, number, expiry date and name and address where the card is registered.